East Coast Hospitality

EAST COAST
THEOLOGY
~
by ACADIA DIVINITY COLLEGE

Ministry in Atlantic Canada can be tough. The challenges our pastors and churches face are not exclusive to us, but they are uniquely shaped and nuanced by our local context. Ministering effectively requires a deep understanding of this place and time, as well as the theological skills to think critically and deeply.

Acadia Divinity College (ADC) is committed to making a fresh impact on issues that are important to life in Atlantic Canada by offering an informed voice from our own perspective. As part of our strategic vision Change with Purpose, ADC has launched a series of books entitled East Coast Theology. This communal publishing project by our faculty focuses on relevant issues shaped by our people, culture, and history. It is a project to collectively discover and shape a theology, one that will seek to inspire, encourage, and challenge the way we approach ministry, both here and elsewhere.

SERIES EDITORS:
Anna M. Robbins
Melody Maxwell

Volume One: *Pandemic, Public Health, and the People of God*
Volume Two: *East Coast Hospitality: Myth or Reality?*

East Coast Hospitality

Myth or Reality?

EAST COAST THEOLOGY SERIES

EDITED BY
MELODY MAXWELL

WIPF & STOCK · Eugene, Oregon

EAST COAST HOSPITALITY
Myth or Reality?

EAST COAST THEOLOGY SERIES

Wipf & Stock
An Imprint of Wipf and Stock Publishers
199 W. 8th Ave., Suite 3
Eugene, OR 97401

www.wipfandstock.com

PAPERBACK ISBN: 979-8-3852-2474-6
HARDCOVER ISBN: 979-8-3852-2475-3
EBOOK ISBN: 979-8-3852-2476-0

VERSION NUMBER 04/04/25

The editor wishes to thank:

- International Journal of Caring Sciences for permission to reprint "Arch of Maguerez"
- John Wiley and Sons for permission to reprint "Model for Improvement"
- Orbis Books for permission to reprint "The Praxis Model"

Contents

CONTENTS

Contributors

GRACE WING YI AU is assistant professor of New Testament studies at Acadia Divinity College. She is also the director of the Master of Arts in Theology program. Originally from Hong Kong, she now lives in Wolfville, Nova Scotia, with her husband, daughter, and cats.

GLEN BERRY has been practicing clinical psychology for over twenty-five years. He is the William and Virginia Leach Associate Professor of Pastoral Psychology and the director of the Charles J. Taylor Centre for Chaplaincy and Spiritual Care at Acadia Divinity College.

SPENCER BOERSMA is an associate professor of theology at Acadia Divinity College. He lives in Kentville, Nova Scotia, with his wife, Meagan, and their five boys.

CHRIS KILLACKY teaches theology at Acadia Divinity College. His background includes education, and he worked in the corporate and public service sectors prior to becoming an academic.

CARLEY LEE is a freelance writer and editor, and she serves as part-time communications coordinator at Acadia Divinity College from her home in Moncton, New Brunswick. She has a diploma in Creative Writing from Oxford University (2018) and a masters in writing for young people from Bath Spa University (2020).

CONTRIBUTORS

JODY LINKLETTER serves as assistant professor of next generation ministries, registrar, and manager of admissions at Acadia Divinity College. Currently, she lives on Prince Edward Island with her husband and daughter and loves their many adventures together.

MELODY MAXWELL serves as associate professor of Christian history at Acadia Divinity College. She also directs the Acadia Centre for Baptist and Anabaptist Studies as well as the International Conference on Baptist Studies.

STEVE MCMULLIN is professor emeritus and consultant on intercultural competency at Acadia Divinity College. He lives in Saint John, New Brunswick, where he is active at RiverCross Church, a historic Baptist congregation now comprised of people from many cultural backgrounds.

D. STEVEN PORTER is assistant professor of church innovation and evangelism and director of doctoral studies at Acadia Divinity College, following thirty years of service as a missionary, educator, and denominational leader. He lives with his family in Wolfville, Nova Scotia.

JODI L. PORTER serves at Acadia Divinity College as director of education for ministry innovation, overseeing the Futuring Lab, and as adjunct faculty. She holds an EdD in leadership and learning in organizations from Peabody College, Vanderbilt University; an MTh in applied (practical) theology from Regent's Park College, University of Oxford; and a BA in Oxbridge honors religious studies from William Jewell College.

ANNA ROBBINS serves as president of Acadia Divinity College and dean of theology for Acadia University. She lives in Wolfville, Nova Scotia, with her husband Peter, son David, and goldendoodle Gatsby.

H. DANIEL ZACHARIAS is a Cree-Anishinaabe/Métis and Austrian man originally from Winnipeg, Manitoba (Treaty One territory). Danny lives in Wolfville, Nova Scotia, with his wife and four children and serves as the associate dean and professor of New Testament studies at Acadia Divinity College.

Series Foreword

ANNA ROBBINS
President, Acadia Divinity College

IT IS MY JOY to introduce the East Coast Theology series. The goal of this series is to explore theology within a specific context: the East Coast of Canada. Students, churches, and their leaders have rarely been equipped with theological resources characterized by academic excellence and a commitment to the local church as it exists in an Atlantic Canadian setting. Our unique landscape, history, and culture inspire our theological reflection and practical ministry to engage with both the Bible and the issues of life on Canada's East Coast. We desire to be intentional about doing theology in the place where we find ourselves and from where we speak to others who wish to hear. I believe that we have something to learn from this intentionality for our life of faith and to share with those who live inside and outside of Atlantic Canada.

We engage the world in particular and nuanced ways in light of our shared life in this place of natural beauty, relational warmth, and conflicted history. Jesus walks here through Mi'kma'ki and Africville, on the waters of the Bay of Fundy and in the mountains of Gros Morne. We follow him with the scent of salt on our clothes and earth under our fingers, through the pine forests of Miramichi and the bustling streets of Halifax. Jesus walks *here*. We follow him *here*. The Bible speaks to *our* experiences and nurtures *our* faith.

Today we recognize that there is an Atlantic Canadian voice that can engage the important issues here, where sea meets land and sky.

Doing theology in an East Coast context means being alert to the issues that emerge here and how people respond to them. It means paying attention to a history that recognizes the land of the Mi'kmaq, the original inhabitants and caretakers whose unceded territory remains occupied. It recognizes the terrible expulsion of the Acadians from the land they had peaceably settled and farmed. It notices the bulldozers that ran over Africville, taking away ownership and dignity from a racialized community. Finally, to do theology in an East Coast context means we wrestle together with the Word in the world as settlers, old and new, First Nations, and racialized people.

As the authors of this volume, we are scholars gathered from diverse places, working as colleagues, focused on common goals and purposes. We sit around the faculty circle at Acadia Divinity College, exploring our shared stories and seeking to understand our diverse experiences. We believe theology grows hands and feet for this place out of a circle of trust, and faithful innovation is birthed for theological education and the church.

It is rare to be part of a faculty that brings individual excellence and particular gifts to a collective effort to serve today's church. Undertaking a series like this would be impossible if we did not enjoy a culture of teamwork and cooperation in the mission we seek to accomplish at Acadia Divinity College. Embracing this unique moment means that we deeply desire to produce something together to engage the world beyond the walls of the church, reflect theologically upon it for the life of the church, and develop a style of doing theology that is rooted in this institution and this land, with these people.

Around our faculty table, diverse voices speak. We tell multiple stories. We listen to one another, and we learn from each other. Yet we share a common faith and purpose, a unique place and time, here on the East Coast.

This is East Coast Theology.

Acknowledgments

MELODY MAXWELL

WITH A PROJECT OF this magnitude, thanks are due to a number of individuals. First, I would like to express my gratitude to Anna Robbins, whose vision led to the creation of the East Coast Theology series. (Volume 1, *Pandemic, Public Health, and the People of God*, is available from Wipf and Stock.) I am also exceedingly grateful to Todd Scoville, recent MA graduate of Acadia Divinity College, whose work ethic and attention to detail are second to none. Todd's copyediting and administrative skills held together this project.

Thanks are due to the authors of each chapter of East Coast Theology, who set aside time from their busy schedules to think and write. The faculty of ADC is also grateful for the time and expertise of Dr. Ray Ivany, who spoke with us about immigration and hospitality in Nova Scotia in preparation for the writing of this volume.

Many individuals were involved in the creation of this book. Thanks go to Berdene Owen for creating the graphics used inside the volume, and to Nicole LaPierre for the volume's cover photo. We are grateful for the efforts of the staff at Wipf and Stock in producing this book. It was a pleasure to work with Matthew Wimer, George Callihan, Rebecca Abbott, Calvin Jaffarian, and Mike Surber. We also thank the team at ADC, especially Carley Lee, for their efforts to let others know about the book.

We likewise extend our appreciation to the church members and leaders who consented to interviews for chapter 11, as well as to those who contributed to the authors' thinking in other ways. We hope that this book will prove useful to Christians and churches in Atlantic Canada and beyond, as we think together about extending hospitality to those around us.

Melody Maxwell

Introduction

MELODY MAXWELL

IN AUGUST 1928, A shy German boy named Frederick walked down a gangplank from a steamship, attempting to keep up with his family among the crowded sea of immigrants descending at the port of Halifax in their new country, Canada. When he reached the dock, he was startled to hear a woman greet his parents. Frederick ducked behind his mother's skirt, slowly peering out when he saw that the strange woman was offering him an orange and a piece of butterscotch candy. "Danke," he said, stepping out to see the woman who offered him such treats. Frederick later discovered her name, Helen Quigley, and her mission of welcoming immigrants at the port on behalf of Canadian Baptists. Quigley met hundreds of families like Frederick's over the course of her ministry, guiding them to the resources they needed and to Baptist churches they might join. Her efforts represented Christian hospitality toward newcomers to the East Coast in the early twentieth century.[1]

Although their circumstances changed, Christians living along Canada's East Coast continued welcoming newcomers. When I first arrived in the area in 2018, I was surprised to hear a knock at my door when I was busily unpacking boxes in my new

---

1. The story of Frederick is fictionalized, but Helen Quigley and her ministry to immigrant children and families were real. See "Board of Home Missions," in F. H. Eaton, ed., *United Baptist Year Book of the Maritime Provinces of Canada, 1928* (Truro, NS: News, 1928), 125–26.

home. A neighbour who attended a local church had brought me flowers and maple syrup to welcome me. A few hours later, another church member dropped off some baked goods. Although I had not yet stepped foot into their church, these neighbours welcomed me with the love of Christ. I soon decided to change out of my sweaty moving clothes and smooth my hair back in case another unexpected visitor dropped by!

Situations like these have helped establish the East Coast's reputation for hospitality. Atlantic Canadians are known to be warm and friendly, stopping to take the time to greet neighbours on the street and to give directions to strangers. At least this is the stereotype, which is based at least partly on reality. As a predominantly rural region, Canada's East Coast can exude small-town charm. Even its cities can have a homey feel mostly absent from the bustling streets of Toronto or Vancouver.

But is this hospitality more than skin deep? And does it apply to the thousands of newcomers who have moved to Atlantic Canada in recent years from around the world? The chapters of this book explore these and related questions. They examine whether the famed East Coast hospitality still exists—or ever really existed at all. Is East Coast hospitality a reality or a myth? Does a newcomer arriving in Halifax today from India experience the same welcome that Frederick and his family received a century ago? Or do long-time Atlantic Canadians prefer to keep to themselves, avoiding the "come from aways" who some feel have invaded their home?

This book explores such questions through a Christian lens. The authors—faculty and staff members at Acadia Divinity College—examine biblical, theological, and practical perspectives on hospitality, asking thought-provoking questions while avoiding easy answers. Multiple chapters discuss hospitality to newcomers, including refugees. Others focus on historical examples of hospitality or the modern-day practices of hospitality seen in local congregations. Some chapters have differing viewpoints on Christian hospitality; this should make for thoughtful conversations for groups who read the book together. Questions are provided at the end of each chapter for such discussions.

Throughout the pages of the book, it is clear that in today's changing world, hospitality is more important than ever for Christians on the East Coast—and beyond—to consider. Regardless of the reputation of the place where we live, as followers of Christ we are called to welcome others and fellowship with them. May we demonstrate countercultural hospitality to the extent that Christians on the East Coast and around the world become known for loving and giving generously to others.

1

"Savage" Hospitality

Why Being Welcomed Matters

H. DANIEL ZACHARIAS

"SAVAGE" HAS HISTORICALLY BEEN a derogatory term, primarily aimed at Indigenous peoples throughout the world. Indigenous peoples were seen as "uncivilized" and more primitive than European settlers. In its earliest usage, "savage" was applied to land and country that was seen as wild, uncultivated, and brutal. In this word and its application, we see the realities of early Indigenous worldviews and lifeways that were deeply connected with their lands. At the same time, we see how colonizing forces viewed the land as a commodity, something that was "savage" and needed to be dominated, and viewed Indigenous peoples as equally "savage" and needing to be dominated. This "othering" of Indigenous peoples helped to justify taking native lands through treaty (sometimes fair, more often forced and coercive), through conquest, or through forced removal. The application of the word to Indigenous peoples is ubiquitous in historical documentation in the early colonial period within Canada and the United States. While the word "savage" has rightly fallen out of usage, the remnants of it still

1

survive in surnames within family lines of Indigenous heritage, as well as through displays like the tomahawk chop at sporting events where teams have native-related names. The Roman Empire at the time of Jesus, and earlier into the Greek period, also had a standard pejorative term used for peoples they considered more primitive: *barbaros*, or barbarian, in Greek.

Yet, despite the perceived incivility of these peoples, we have countless examples of "savage hospitality" from history and from our sacred text. In this essay, I want to look at three examples: one from historical sources related to Turtle Island (North America) and two from Scripture. From these examples, I ask what it means to think about ourselves as ones who are welcomed. Hospitality is an important virtue, and a life characterized by hospitality ought to be commonplace within the church of Christ. But sometimes, flipping the script is important. When we hear the word "hospitality" today, I wager that believers almost always think about something *we should do*—and certainly, it is something we should do. But I want to suggest that the Scripture also places an emphasis on being *the recipient* of hospitality.

THE ORIGINAL "SAVAGE"

As noted above, "savage" originally applied to the land. My first example of "savage hospitality" is the land itself. In the Hebrew creation narrative of Gen 1, God creates a home for all of his creatures, including us. Humanity and our fellow creatures are made to rely on the gifts of the land, as it is the land that creates the vegetation that will feed us (vv. 11–12). Verses 29–30 are particularly important, as we see that the vegetation of the land is given to air and land creatures (including us) as food. Only after we are placed within an ongoing relationship with the community of creation around us does God declare things as "very good" (v. 31 NRSV). As we move to Gen 2, we see Creator place our first parents in the garden of Eden. It is this garden that is meant to sustain Adam and Eve; they are "to serve and conform to her" (v. 15 translation mine). The creation stories in Genesis show that part of what it means to be human is to be hosted.

Because part of what it means to be human is to be hosted, it is no surprise that we see the Lord Jesus being hosted as well. Most of us are familiar with the gospel stories of Jesus hosted by people in their homes, and indeed Jesus and his disciples were hosted and cared for by a circle of female disciples (Mark 15:41; Luke 10:38–41). But before his time of ministry, Jesus, as the truly human one, first received hospitality from the "original savage." All of creation welcomed Jesus at the incarnation. In Luke, this is represented by the angelic host and the lowly shepherds joining the welcome alongside his family and the animals that were inevitably around the feeding trough (Luke 2:1–20). The Gospel of John, though, theologically reflects on the incarnation of Jesus rather than providing a narrative of Jesus' birth. As part of the prologue, the evangelist makes it clear that "the world came into being through him" (1:10 NRSV). John then states, "He came to what was his own, and his own people did not accept him" (1:11 NRSV). This verse has tended to be read by modern commentators as entirely focused on Jesus' humanity, but the previous verse makes it clear that all of creation is in view, not just humanity. The first part of verse 11 in the Greek indicates that Jesus "came to his own [things]," i.e., all that came into being through him. Yet, the second half of the verse indicates that it is the people—humanity—who did not accept him. Just as the first Adam was welcomed in the garden, the second Adam was welcomed by non-human creation.

"SAVAGE" RECEPTION OF THE GOSPEL AND ITS REPRESENTATIVE

As previously mentioned, the ancient equivalent to the modern word "savage" was *barbaros*, the Greek word from which the word "barbarian" derives. Like the use of "savage" in the modern period, *barbaros* was always used of foreigners, indicating what was considered to be their crudeness and incivility. *Barbaros* is used as a category of people by the apostle Paul as he indicates the inclusive reach of Christ to all people: "In that renewal there is no longer Greek and Jew, circumcised and uncircumcised, barbarian, Scythian, slave and free; but Christ is all and in all" (Col 3:11 NRSV). Luke narrates a specific encounter with *barbaroi* (plural) in Acts 28:2. This Greek word is translated in numerous ways within modern translations, with most of them downplaying the denigrative use of the word in the ancient world ("natives" in the NRSV and ESV; "islanders" in the NIV, CEB, and NLT; "local people/inhabitants" in the NET and CSB). Only the original KJV translates the word as "the barbarous people," which best captures the negative aspect that it held. The KJV translation of *barbaros* precisely highlights what Luke is trying to emphasize—even those traditionally considered "the other" are not outside the reach of the gospel's embrace.

What's more, Luke has set the stage for this situation to turn into an inhospitable and dangerous scenario, with Paul and those on the ship being washed up on the island with the wild and uncivilized *barbaroi* (Acts 28:8–9). Yet, according to Joshua Jipp, "Their kindness to the prisoners is, according to prominent Hellenistic moralists, the height of virtue since shipwrecked strangers have no means to reciprocate for hospitality received."[1] It turns out that Paul, God's representative to the non-Jewish world, received "savage hospitality." The reception of hospitality from "the other" becomes a means of grace for Paul and his companions and opens the door for the ministry of Jesus through Paul to come to the island. As Paul parts with the natives of the island, he does so by means of their generosity. Jipp suggests that Luke intends to show that a binding relationship has begun between the apostle and the people: "The Maltese barbarians, then, through their continued enactments of hospitality, appear to have initiated a binding kinship-like relationship with Paul."[2]

Important implications can be drawn from this passage as Christians strive towards missional living in our contexts. The emphasis on individualism and independence within modern

---

1. Jipp, *Saved by Faith*, 104.
2. Jipp, *Saved by Faith*, 106.

society has sometimes hampered our ability to receive hospitality, and the exhortation to hospitality in the church today is often heard as an exhortation to *provide* hospitality. Yet, in this example, it was in the reception of hospitality that the gospel could take root in a new context and new bonds of kinship formed. In some sense, Paul could be viewed as enacting Jesus' instructions to the twelve disciples in Matt 10:5–15. These instructions placed the Twelve as both recipients of hospitality in people's homes and givers of ministry and healing wherever they found themselves. Despite the prominence of the Great Commission at the end of the Gospel of Matthew, the instructions to the Twelve in Matt 10:5–15 provide more detailed instructions on how to "go forth and make disciples." Central to these instructions was the disciple first receiving hospitality. This posture of need and reliance is an important component of missional living.

"SAVAGE" HOSPITALITY ON TURTLE ISLAND

The arrival of European settlers on Turtle Island, specifically the East Coast of Canada, introduced a new dynamic to Indigenous peoples' long-standing relationships with their lands and each other. While settlers often categorized the Indigenous peoples as "savage" and uncivilized, the historical record shows a complex and nuanced interaction, characterized at times by Indigenous communities extending a warm welcome and essential hospitality. This hospitality was integral to the survival of many early European arrivals.

The French and other European settlers who arrived in the sixteenth and seventeenth centuries would have struggled to survive without the assistance and hospitality of the Indigenous peoples they encountered. Jacques Cartier's expeditions in the 1530s offer early examples. In 1534, Cartier noted that Indigenous people in what is now Prince Edward Island approached his crew with signs of friendship, offering goods for trade, including animal skins. Despite language barriers, the Indigenous peoples made their desire for peaceful interaction clear, greeting the explorers with gestures of hospitality.[3] These exchanges, although brief, marked the beginning of a series of interactions where Indigenous peoples helped newcomers understand the land and its resources. One of the most well-documented acts of Indigenous hospitality occurred with the Mi'kmaq, who played a significant role in helping newcomers navigate the harsh realities of the Canadian climate and wilderness. French settlers relied heavily on the Mi'kmaq for their knowledge of survival techniques, such as how to fish and hunt in unfamiliar terrain.[4] In one instance, Mi'kmaq guides helped Pierre du Gua de Monts and Samuel de Champlain explore and map the region, showing them where to find resources like copper and guiding them along the waterways of Nova Scotia.[5] The Mi'kmaq welcomed and assisted French colonists in Port Royal in the early seventeenth century, a relationship that continued even in times of trouble. During the Acadian expulsion by the British, the Mi'kmaq stayed faithful to their relationship with the Acadians. As one source puts it,

> Acadian culture was almost extinguished, except for the audacious and timely rescue of numerous Acadians by the Mi'kmaq. And throughout the dense forest wilderness, Acadians were fed, clothed, and sheltered in the wigwams of the Mi'kmaq, safe from the clutches of the British soldiers. The Mi'kmaq had assured the survival of the Acadian culture in North America.[6]

The hospitality the Mi'kmaq and other Indigenous groups offered was not only material but also cultural. Indigenous peoples often shared food, shelter, and knowledge with the settlers, teaching them essential skills like using medicinal plants and navigating dense forests. In turn, the French introduced items such as metal tools, which became highly prized by most First Nations. The French, particularly through their interactions with the Mi'kmaq, embraced aspects of Indigenous culture and engaged in gift-giving

3. Whitehead, *Old Man Told Us*, 9–10.

4. Ray, *Illustrated History*, 46–48.

5. Whitehead, *Old Man Told Us*, 22–23.

6. Sark and Pollard, *Spirit World*, 26:18.

practices that were central to maintaining harmonious relationships. This cultural exchange was exemplified by the relationship between the French explorers and the Mi'kmaq leader Membertou, who became an important intermediary between the two groups. Membertou's welcoming of the French and his eventual conversion to Catholicism were pivotal moments that illustrated the depth of the exchange between the two cultures.[7]

While initial encounters were often marked by cooperation and mutual support, tensions inevitably arose as settlers sought to claim land and resources. The Indigenous understanding of land as communal and sacred clashed with the European view of land as a commodity to be owned and exploited. However, even in the face of these growing tensions, many Indigenous groups continued to extend hospitality to European settlers. The Mi'kmaq, for instance, maintained trade relationships with the French, providing them with pelts and other goods in exchange for European wares despite the increasing pressures of colonization. At the same time, Indigenous peoples were not passive in their relationships with Europeans. They engaged strategically, using diplomacy and sometimes withdrawing their hospitality as a means of resistance. An example of this was the shift in Mi'kmaq attitudes towards the French after realizing the long-term impact of European diseases and settlement on their populations. They initially welcomed the French, but over time, the Mi'kmaq became more cautious in their interactions, recognizing the threat posed by the newcomers.

The hospitality extended by Indigenous peoples, especially on the East Coast of Canada, was instrumental in the establishment and survival of European settlements. Without the generosity and guidance of Indigenous communities, many early colonies would have failed. This "savage" hospitality was a powerful demonstration of the relational worldview held by Indigenous peoples—prioritizing community, reciprocity, and the care of the land and its inhabitants. In the broader narrative of colonization, these early acts of hospitality are often overshadowed by the subsequent conflicts and dispossession that Indigenous peoples

7. Whitehead, *Old Man Told Us*, 26, 33.

faced. However, understanding these moments of welcome helps to reframe the story, highlighting the agency and generosity of Indigenous peoples.

LESSONS FROM BEING WELCOMED

As we move ahead to the future portraits in the Scriptures, we see that we will once again be recipients of the hospitality of God and of creation. Whether it be Revelation's "marriage supper of the lamb" (19:9 NRSV; 19:17), the banquet with the patriarchs and matriarchs described by Jesus (Matt 8:11; Matt 22:1–18), or Isaiah's messianic banquet with "rich food" and "well-aged wines" (25:6–8 NRSV), our life with God is characterized by being hosted. In the New Testament, there is a strong theme of divine hospitality in the Gospel of John, as Jesus gives himself as living water (John 4:10), as bread (6:35), and as shepherd and gate for the sheep (10:7, 11). He also washes the disciples' feet (13:5). All of this is in preparation for yet further hospitality, as Jesus prepares us to join God's family in the rooms the Father has prepared for us (14:2).

In all these stories, God and Christ are the givers of hospitality, and the originator of hospitality is God. As we provide hospitality to one another, we are imitating the character of God and conforming ourselves to the image of Christ. But God and Christ are also *recipients* of hospitality in the Scriptures. An example from Gen 18 is when three "men" approach Abraham. Abraham and Sarah proceed to provide hospitality to these three strangers. While there has been some debate as to the identity of these three visitors, a number of Genesis scholars argue that they are God and two angels, or that the narrative, at the very least, is intentionally ambiguous. But the beginning of the story indicates a divine visitation: "The LORD appeared to Abraham by the oaks of Mamre, as he sat at the entrance of his tent in the heat of the day" (vv. 1–2 NRSV). Numerous examples in the ministry of Christ also show that he received hospitality and support from others. He ate in the home of others like Zacchaeus (Luke 19:5–9), relied on the kindness of Mary, Martha, and Lazarus when in the Jerusalem area

(Luke 10:38–42), and was known to dine frequently with "sinners" (Mark 2:16 NRSV). If God and Christ both give *and* receive hospitality, then receiving hospitality is something that can help us be both more human and more Christlike.

By applying the examples provided in this chapter, the "savage" hospitality continually given by creation should orient all of humanity in important ways because it will make us more authentically human and more authentically Christlike. We could not exist without the gifts of the community of creation. This sacrificial act of hospitality reminds us that the nature of humanity is to be cared for by creation. This initiates, or ought to initiate, an ongoing relationship of reciprocity in which we serve and conform to lands we occupy—just like our first parents were to do in the garden.

The example of "savage" hospitality in Acts 28 helps us challenge labels and caricatures that continue to plague humanity, especially in polarized societies. Just as *barbaros* was used in the Roman empire to demean, dehumanize, and "other" groups of people, modern labels today like "woke," "fundamentalist," and "critical race theory" can be simple ways to reduce humans and other them. The story in Acts of Paul in Malta challenges us not simply to avoid these labels but also to be recipients of hospitality from the "cultural other." Not only will this open up networks and foster unlikely new relationships, but these very connections will also foster the spread of God's good news. The example of Paul on Malta especially reminds us of the importance of respecting others' agency when you are in their land and space. Much like Jesus' instructions to the Twelve when he sent them out to do ministry (Matt 10:5–15), Paul and his companions were to be first welcomed into a home—i.e., receive hospitality—before launching into proclamation and ministry. This has important implications for missions and was a lesson that was sadly not learned during the European colonization of Turtle Island.

As noted previously, the hospitality of Indigenous peoples was literally a matter of life and death for some of the earliest European settlers. Friendships and alliances formed, and the earliest treaties—including the Peace and Friendship Treaties that continue to govern the East Coast of Canada—were about the generous sharing of land and resources. Unfortunately, these earliest encounters included a clash of worldviews and cultures. The Indigenous people understood what it meant to have overlapping sovereignties within a shared space because the concept of land ownership was foreign to them. The colonial settlers came with the assumption of land ownership and could not fathom overlapping sovereignties, especially with the spiritual authority of the Doctrine of Discovery bolstering their monarch's claim over "heathen" lands. (The Doctrine of Discovery was a legal and religious framework originating in the fifteenth century, which granted European Christian explorers the right to claim lands they "discovered" and assert dominance over non-Christian inhabitants.) As unknown diseases began to ravage Indigenous peoples and as the balance of numbers (and therefore power) of settlers rose, the hospitality and initial treaties of shared spaces were forgotten, and Indigenous peoples became the "other." They were problems to be solved, and people to be cleared out for European expansion. And for the church, they were, and in many cases continue to be, "still just a mission field."[8]

We have been recipients of "savage" hospitality, both individually and corporately. There are important lessons to learn from being welcomed, lessons that we have not always learned or have quickly forgotten. And perhaps this is even important enough to warrant its own theological label—*ortholempsis*. Theologians speak of orthodoxy—right belief. They speak of orthopathy—the right ordering of our hearts, desires, and emotions. And they speak of orthopraxy—the right action and practice in light of our Christian commitments. The giving of hospitality certainly sits within orthopraxy. But this essay has shown the importance of also being the receiver, *ortholempsis*—with *lempsis* being the Greek noun for "receive." In light of the essays in this volume, the many teachings on hospitality in the Scriptures, our own experiences of being welcomed, and the ongoing reconciliation efforts stemming from the Truth and Reconciliation Commission, my

8. Twiss, *One Church*, 58.

hope is that we would learn and lean into the relationships of reciprocity that ought to blossom when we are hosted. May we practice *ortholempsis*—rightly ordering our receiving.

SUGGESTIONS FOR FURTHER READING

Jipp, Joshua W. *Saved by Faith and Hospitality*. Grand Rapids: Eerdmans, 2017.

Ray, Arthur J. *An Illustrated History of Canada's Native People: I Have Lived Here Since the World Began*. 4th ed. Montreal: McGill-Queen's University Press, 2011.

Sark, John Joe, and Brian Pollard. *Spirit World, the Story of the Mi'kmaq*. Charlottetown, Can.: Mi'kmaq Pictures and Vision TV, 2003. https://youtu.be/vSduTaTPsME?si=XKvVgIhtgQyexTw_.

Woodley, Randy S. *Mission and the Cultural Other: A Closer Look*. Eugene, OR: Cascade, 2022.

Zacharias, H. Daniel. "The Land Takes Care of Us: Recovering Creator's Relational Design." In *Theologies of Land: Contested Land, Spatial Justice, and Identity*, edited by K. K. Yeo and Gene L. Green, 69–97. Crosscurrents in Majority World and Minority Theology. Eugene, OR: Cascade, 2020.

BIBLIOGRAPHY

Jipp, Joshua W. *Saved by Faith and Hospitality*. Grand Rapids: Eerdmans, 2017.

Ray, Arthur J. *An Illustrated History of Canada's Native People: I Have Lived Here Since the World Began*. 4th ed. Montreal: McGill-Queen's University Press, 2011.

Sark, John Joe, and Brian Pollard. *Spirit World, the Story of the Mi'kmaq*. Charlottetown, Can.: Mi'kmaq Pictures and Vision TV, 2003. https://youtu.be/vSduTaTPsME?si=XKvVgIhtgQyexTw_.

Twiss, Richard. *One Church, Many Tribes: Following Jesus the Way God Made You*. Minneapolis: Chosen, 2000.

Whitehead, Ruth Holmes. *The Old Man Told Us: Excerpts from Mi'kmaw History 1500–1950*. Halifax, NS: Nimbus, 1991.

DISCUSSION QUESTIONS

1. The chapter emphasizes the importance of being both givers and receivers of hospitality. How does the biblical narrative of creation (Gen 1–2) shape our understanding of being "hosted" by the land? How might this influence our relationship with the environment today?

2. The term "savage" was historically used to demean Indigenous peoples, yet their acts of hospitality were vital to the survival of early European settlers. How does this challenge contemporary views of the "other," and what lessons can Christians draw from the Indigenous example of hospitality?

3. The chapter draws parallels between Paul's reception by the *barbaroi* in Acts 28 and Indigenous hospitality in Canada. How does being a recipient of hospitality from those we consider "outsiders" reshape our understanding of missional living and the spread of the gospel?

4. In what ways does the scriptural model of receiving hospitality (e.g., the stories of Jesus and the Twelve) offer insights into how Christians should engage in relationships, both within their communities and in intercultural contexts today?

2

"Welcome One Another as Christ Has Welcomed Us"

From the Other to One Another in Romans 14–15

GRACE WING YI AU

AMONG THE ARTIFACTS ARCHIVED at the Canadian Museum of Immigration at Pier 21 in Halifax, Nova Scotia, one statement stood out: "If one thing caused scenes at Pier 21, it was sausages."[1] Ilse Koerner, a German immigrant who arrived in Halifax aboard the SS *Conte Biancamano* from Genoa, Italy, on June 22, 1954, recalled the scene. Food confiscated from newcomers was "piled up in a heap in the middle of the hall. Rays of sunshine painted a colourful still of that mountain of sausages, loaves of bread, wheels of cheeses, fruits and other perishable items."[2] Food and its confiscation turned the pier into a battleground between immigrants' fears of losing their cherished memories of their homelands and Canadian officials' desire to protect Canadian society from diseases

1. Raska, "Food Wars!," para. 1.
2. Raska, "Anything to Declare?," para. 6.

from around the world. Newcomers often went to great lengths to conceal their beloved food products from Canadian customs officers. The pile of confiscated food not only revealed what the immigrants ate or that the food they were accustomed to was not available in Canada; it also represented how the newcomers transplanted their cultural heritage into a new country. For newcomers, culinary traditions often bind together individual and family identities, becoming a link to their past. It is not only "you are what you eat," but more importantly, "you are who you eat with." The food hidden in the immigrants' luggage distilled the essence of their cultural memories, their sense of comfort and security, not to mention their ethno-religious backgrounds.

Yes, you are reading a chapter in the East Coast Theology series. More than biological, nutritional, and individual acts of food consumption, meals are cultural, psychological, and social practices. In its early history, Christianity was a distinct socioreligious phenomenon that took shape at the table. Sometimes, food has a special way of bringing people together and strengthening fellowship around the table. But sometimes, just like the pile of confiscated food at Pier 21, food can be a source of disagreement, dispute, and discord. Romans 14:1—15:13 is one such example.

After briefly describing the sociohistorical background of the dispute discussed in this passage and the identity of the two parties, I will elaborate on the problem the passage considers and the detrimental effect of this judgment, as Paul recognizes. Instead of taking sides, Paul turns the question of judgment over food into a question of relationship, challenging us to see one another as fellow brothers and sisters or household servants who belong to the same master. The theology of "other-regarding" mutuality is finally realized in Paul's prayer and praise—so that with one mind and one voice we may glorify the God and Father of our Lord Jesus Christ.

THE TWO PARTIES

In this passage, Paul explicitly addresses practical issues in every-day life in the early churches in Rome. It is not hard to imagine that the identity of the "strong" and the "weak" in these verses is an unsettled issue among scholars. Identifying the "strong" as Christ-believing gentiles is less controversial than linking the "weak" to either Jewish Christ believers, other gentile Christ believers who lived a Jewish lifestyle, or both. Although the boundary may be more fluid than dividing the two groups simply by ethnic origin, it is sufficient for our purposes to recognize that the issue here most likely reflects a division along Jewish-gentile lines. The opening of the passage sets the scene for disagreements: those whose "faith is weak" (14:1 NIV) abstain from meat (14:2) and probably from wine dedicated to idols (14:21), and they honor the Sabbath, Jewish feasts, or fasts (14:5–6) according to *kosher* rules (14:14, 20). In contrast, all foods and all days are acceptable for the "strong" (14:2, 5). The problem partly overlaps with 1 Cor 8–10. Although Paul does not mention meat sacrificed to idols (1 Cor 8:1) but refers in Rom 14–15 to food and wine in general, eating meat brought from the market still risked consuming unclean food in Jewish terms, either because it was associated with every-day idolatry, or not prepared according to Jewish *kosher* practice (Dan 1:8–16). In any case, the dispute is about the extent to which certain practices of the Mosaic law should be integrated with faith in Christ. Obviously, it is not a problem that can be solved simply by adding a few vegan dishes or setting aside a separate table for vegetarians at the church potluck.

THE DANGER OF JUDGING

The question of the table is not a matter of taste but of ideology. The contention is vividly described in a series of *kri*-words. The Greek *kri*-stem is evident in the passage: dispute (*dia<u>kri</u>seis* [14:1]), judging (*<u>kri</u>nein* [14:3, 4, 5, 10, 13, 22]), having doubts (*dia<u>kri</u>nein* [14:23]), and condemning (*kata<u>kri</u>nein* [14:23]). There is a heavy preponderance of judgment-related words, such as "to regard" (14:6 NIV) and "to approve" (14:22 NIV). The etymological link with the English word "criticism" is hard to miss. For Paul, the language of perceptions and convictions expresses the pernicious problem of human judgment in disputes. What was happening in Romans still sounds familiar today.

In *Age of Anger: A History of the Present*, Pankaj Mishra, inspired by his observations in 2017, offers a precise but pessimistic account of our global crisis. He argues that under the old Western-dominated neoliberal world order, the burden of survival as a self-sustained, highly competitive modern individual has proven too much for many. The feeling of being coerced and humiliated by global elites can turn into hatred and distrust of those closest to you. The age of anger in which we find ourselves is characterized by an "endemic and uncontrollable" violence fueled by a range of hatreds—of "immigrants, minorities and various designated 'others'"—that have now become part of the political mainstream. In Mishra's own words, "The result is, as Arendt feared, a 'tremendous increase in mutual hatred and a somewhat universal irritability of everybody against everybody else' . . . an existential resentment of other people's being, caused by an intense mix of envy and sense of humiliation and powerlessness, *ressentiment*, as it lingers and deepens, poisons civil society and undermines political liberty, and is presently making for a global turn to authoritarianism and toxic forms of chauvinism."[3] The diverse group of Christ followers in Rome lived in a very different political context, of course. But their resentments may not have been so different.

Is there a way out when people with polarized sociopolitical or cultural views are so deeply stuck in their ways? A year after Mishra, American missiologist Ed Stetzer expressed his gospel-centered wish in his book *Christians in the Age of Outrage: How to Bring Our Best When the World Is at Its Worst*. As a prolific participant in social media conversations, Stetzer encourages Christians to bring their faith into digital conversations. Among many insights, Stetzer recognizes how social media has become a

3. Mishra, *Age of Anger*, 14.

place where people, including Christians, become nastier. It can be a brewing cauldron of rage. Rather than facilitating civil dialogue between different perspectives, the echo chamber created by social media discourse contributes to polarization, dehumanization, and, worst of all, the normalization of hatred. Studies suggest that social media users tend to reaffirm existing beliefs, emphasize the distance between their in-group and members of the out-group, and become awash in anger, division, and hostility.[4] Stetzer puts it succinctly: "Outrage is motivated by a desire to punish or destroy rather than reconcile and refine."[5] Stetzer's words echo Paul's warnings: "Do not by your eating destroy someone for whom Christ died" (14:15 NIV); "Do not destroy the work of God for the sake of food" (14:20 NIV); and "It is better not to eat meat or drink wine or to do anything else that will cause your brother or sister to fall" (14:21 NIV; see also 14:13). The destructive power of the flesh is on full display in our judgmental words, whether in our daily or digital lives.

TWO QUESTIONS THAT REDEFINE

Although Paul's admonitions throughout the passage are in second-person plural pronouns—addressing "you all"—two rhetorical questions in chapter 14 stand out by using two second-person singular pronouns ("you"):

> Who are you to judge someone else's servant? To their own master, servants stand or fall. And they will stand, for the Lord is able to make them stand. (v. 4 NIV)

> You, then, why do you judge your brother or sister? . . . For we will all stand before God's judgment seat. (v. 10 NIV)

Imagine Paul entering the heated online anonymous debate forum in these Roman churches and asking everyone involved to reveal their true identities. He asks, "Who are you? . . . Why do you

---

4. Harel et al., "Normalization of Hatred," 2–3.

5. Stetzer, *Christians in the Age*, 80.

judge?" Paul is not just finding fault with everyone. He is asking a completely different question. Instead of asking, "Which camp do you support, the strong or the weak?," Paul asks each of us: "What is your relationship with each other?" For Paul, the question of the table is not a question of taste, and it is not a question of ideology. It is a question of relationship. It does not matter which camp you belong to; the "other" is not an abstract idea. He or she is God's servant. He or she is your brother or sister. Paul challenges us to look at one another as "siblings" (14:10, 13, 15, 21) or as "household slaves" who belong to the same master: Christ. The answers to these rhetorical questions further illustrate Paul's point:

> To their own master, servants stand or fall. And they will stand, for the Lord is able to make them stand. (v. 4 NIV)

> For we will all stand before God's judgment seat. (v. 10 NIV)

Paul's ethic has a theological dimension that extends beyond the relationships between all Roman church members, Jews and gentiles alike. One's brother or sister is identified in relation to God. He or she is God's servant, standing before God's judgment seat, just like you. This fellow Christian is further defined in relation to the identity-shaping event on the cross: He or she is someone "for whom Christ died" (14:15 NIV) and "the work of God" (14:20 NIV). Judgment is not a matter of reflecting in isolation on what is right and wrong, but a pattern of relationship. Judgment against "someone's" [God's] household "servant" (14:4 NIV), who is also your fellow brother or sister (14:10), is banned because there is only one judge—God—who is able to make us stand or fall. Therefore, the argument that takes place at the table does not simply hurt feelings or irritate individuals (14:15); it has consequences for salvation (14:20). To judge or despise one another is to impose a measure of worth that is contrary to God's measure of worth.[6] For Paul, the question of the table is not just a question of taste, not just a question of ideology, not even just a question of personal relationship; it is ultimately a question of theology.

6. Au, *Paul's Designations of God*, 177–78.

Although we have referred to the two groups described in this passage in the conventional terms of "weak" and "strong," our English translation cannot fully convey the nuance of the Greek. The differences between the two groups are framed in terms of faith throughout Rom 14: one person believes that one can eat anything, rendered "one person's faith allows them to eat anything" (v. 2 NIV), while the one whose "faith is weak" eats only vegetables (vv. 1–2 NIV). It is not until Rom 15 that Paul highlights their difference in terms of *power*. The term "strong" is used for the first time in 15:1 (NIV), describing such people not as "strong in faith" but literally as "the powerful ones" (*hoi dunatoi*). In similar terms, the other party is "the powerless" (*hoi adunatoi*). Interestingly, the related Greek verb "being able to" (*dunatein*) is used to describe God who is able to cause his servant to stand or fall in 14:4, as discussed above. Paul highlights the powerful party in 15:1 (NIV) and exhorts us to "bear with the failings of the weak and not to please ourselves." He suddenly uses the first-person plural pronoun to include himself in the scene. Sometimes, interpreters argue that Paul is endorsing the position of the "strong." However, I believe it is unlikely that Paul openly sided with the judgment of one party at the expense of another immediately after giving a long warning against judging and despising. Given that Paul had never visited Rome at the time of the letter, I agree with John Barclay that Paul "would hardly donate his authority as a blank cheque cashable by any Pauline group claiming to be 'the strong.'"[7] If it is true that Paul is not interested in commenting on who is right and who is wrong, what is his theological answer?

Paul does not adopt the label "powerful" to mark his readers' superiority over the powerless. He advocates, I believe, a theology of mutuality and accommodation. In ancient Roman society, Jewish eating habits were one of the reasons Jews were slandered and accused. It is not hard to imagine that the reproaches and derision directed at Christ-following Jews in Rome would be shared by the majority of gentile Christians if they had to go vegan in their communal meals. This was a costly solidarity with the powerless.

7. Barclay, *Jews in Mediterranean Diaspora*, 289.

Both commands in 15:1–2 are addressed to the powerful. Indeed, Paul has been addressing the "faith havers" since 14:13. They are required to accommodate the cultural practices of the weak or the powerless. Otherwise, eating is considered bad because it causes the brother and sister to stumble (14:13, 20, 21; 1 Cor 8:9–13). The heavy burden of change is placed on the shoulders of the powerful. The instruction to please one's neighbour is further elaborated in 15:2 with two purposes: for the good of others and the upbuilding of the church. The idea of "building up" is not only a natural opposition to destroying God's work (14:20), but it also recalls Paul's earlier call to pursue peace and mutual upbuilding (14:19). Metaphorical language about the edification of God's church is not unusual in Paul's letters (e.g., 1 Cor 3:9; 14:3, 5, 12). Paul encourages Christians to regard each other well, not just to bring harmony but also because of the spiritual benefits to the church. Perhaps Paul knows he is asking a lot from the powerful; he appeals to the example of Christ in the next step of his discourse—"for even Christ did not please himself" (15:3 NIV). Reading alongside 14:17–20, the ideas of mutual upbuilding and regarding the "other" are connected to well-pleasing service to Christ.

A UNIFIED COMMUNITY OF WORSHIPPERS

In 15:5–6 (NIV), Paul elevates the communal issue at the table to the level of worship with two prayers to support his argument, which focuses on God. Paul concludes with the prayer:

> May the God who gives endurance and encouragement give you the same attitude of mind toward each other that Christ Jesus had, so that with one mind and one voice you may glorify the God and Father of our Lord Jesus Christ.

The words "each other" recall 14:13 (NIV), where Paul admonished against "passing judgment on one another." The same word is translated as "mutual" in 14:19 (NIV) to refer to mutual edification. The only values that do not destroy but build up "one another" are righteousness, peace, and joy in the Spirit (14:17–19). Fellow believers are welcomed to the meal (14:3) because everyone stands before God based on Christ's welcome alone (15:7). The believers' new "standing," as discussed above, echoes Paul's earlier idea of "this grace in which we now stand" (Rom 5:2 NIV). The correspondence between Rom 5:1–5 and 14:1—15:13 illustrated below may reinforce the suggestion that Paul takes up the core values in his later exhortation:

	Rom 5:1–5 NIV	Rom 14:1—15:13 NIV
peace	5:1	14:17, 19
through faith	5:1	14:2
stand	5:2	14:4, 10
hope	5:2, 4, 5	15:4, 12, 13 (2x)
the glory of God	5:2	15:7
endurance	5:3, 4	15:4, 5
love	5:5	14:15
Holy Spirit	5:5	14:17; 15:13

Romans 5:1–5 celebrates the new reality created in Christ. Standing in God's grace, we secure hope because endurance and perseverance are formed in the heart transformed by the gift of the Spirit (Rom 2:15, 29). Paul is clear that the solidarity he is praying for is not a human achievement but God's gift. Harmony is more than mutual tolerance or the absence of conflict. Guided by his vision of the gospel, Paul prays that divine perseverance and encouragement will transform individual judgmental minds within the contending churches into the "other-regarding" mind of Christ. The renewed, transformed, and redeemed mind is not a forced unity but a new symphony and harmony expressed in corporate worship (Rom 15:6–7). The unity of mind and voice does not eliminate difference, for it is realized in the universal worship of the divine Other. As Jews and gentiles are welcomed and

accepted by God, divided minds and tongues are transformed into one mind and one voice glorifying God (Rom 15:6). As a result, universal multiethnic worship (Rom 15:7–13) is a physical expression of the post-baptismal life marked by a new standing in Christ. Finger-pointing and tongue-lashing are not stopped by persuasive rhetoric or difficult theological talk; unity is achieved by spiritually transformed minds and mouths in prayer and worship. Prayer and praise explicitly (re)orient us to the divine Other. Cursing lips and deceitful tongues are muted by praises that glorify God (Rom 3:10–17). It is at the table of the divine Other, who welcomes and accepts sinners, that we realize that Jews and gentiles alike are all servants of God, for whom Jesus Christ died.

You may want to accuse Paul of being unfair in asking the powerful to accommodate, or you may want to criticize Paul for not understanding the plight of the powerless, or you may want to complain that Paul cannot give you practical advice on how to deal with disputes in your intercultural Canadian congregation. Fair enough. But if you are tired of the avalanche of criticism, judgment, or opinion, Paul invites you to join him and one another in prayer and praise with a transformed, Christlike mind. Come, let's praise!

I usually do not like to end with stories. Sometimes, stories distract or distort; sometimes, stories just add a few sparks. But here, I will end with a story. A version of the story is found in an article by James French.[8] The first time I heard this story was in a Bible study group. Although I cannot remember the Bible passage, the story lingers. I humbly hope that both Rom 14–15 and the following story will stay with you:

> During a communion service between an affluent church and mission churches in the slums, a former burglar, now a Christian worker, knelt beside the judge who had sentenced him to prison. After the service, the judge commented to the pastor about the scene, calling it a "miracle of grace." When the pastor assumed that the judge was referring to the ex-convict, the judge clarified that he was

8. French, "Religion."

referring to himself. He explained that while it was easier for the burglar to see his need for grace because of his past, it was much harder for someone like him, raised with privilege, to see his equal need for God's grace.

SUGGESTIONS FOR FURTHER READING

Gaventa, Beverly Roberts. *When in Romans: An Invitation to Linger with the Gospel According to Paul.* Grand Rapids: Baker Academic, 2016.
Meeks, Wayne A. "Judgment and the Brother: Romans 14:1—15:13." In *Tradition and Interpretation in the New Testament: Essays in Honor of E. E. Ellis,* edited by Gerald F. Hawthorne and Otto Betz, 290–300. Grand Rapids: Eerdmans, 1987.

BIBLIOGRAPHY

Au, Wing Yi. *Paul's Designations of God in Romans.* Wissenschaftliche Untersuchungen zum Neuen Testament, 2nd ser., 590. Tübingen: Mohr Siebeck, 2023.
Barclay, John M. G. *Jews in the Mediterranean Diaspora: From Alexander to Trajan (323 BC—117 CE).* Hellenistic Culture and Society 33. Edinburgh: T&T Clark, 1996.
French, James "Skip." "Religion: What a Miracle of Grace." *Weekly Vista,* Sept. 23, 2020. https://bvwv.nwaonline.com/news/2020/sep/23/religion-what-a-miracle-of-grace/.
Harel, Tal Orian, et al. "The Normalization of Hatred: Identity, Affective Polarization, and Dehumanization on Facebook in the Context of Intractable Political Conflict." *Social Media + Society* 6 (2020). https://doi.org/10.1177/2056305120913983.
Mishra, Pankaj. *Age of Anger: A History of the Present.* New York: Farrar, Straus and Giroux, 2017.
Raska, Jan. "Anything to Declare? Part 2—Reflections on Immigration and Custom Experiences at Pier 21." Canadian Museum of Immigration at Pier 21, updated Oct. 2, 2020. https://pier21.ca/blog/jan-raska/anything-to-declare-part-2-reflections-on-immigration-and-customs-experiences-at-pier.
———. "Food Wars! Immigration and Food Confiscation at Pier 21." Canadian Museum of Immigration at Pier 21, updated Nov. 5, 2020. https://pier21.ca/blog/jan-raska/food-wars-immigration-and-food-confiscation-at-pier-21.
Stetzer, Ed. *Christians in the Age of Outrage: How to Bring Our Best When the World Is at Its Worst.* Carol Stream, IL: Tyndale, 2018.

DISCUSSION QUESTIONS

1. What do you think about the story of food confiscation at Pier 21? What cultural differences or misunderstandings have led to tensions in a church setting today? How do these differences create challenges or opportunities for unity in a diverse church community?

2. Paul urges Roman believers to shift their focus from judgment to building relationships as brothers and sisters in Christ and servants of the Lord. What lessons can we learn from this when navigating disagreements in our church? How might this change how you relate to one another and how you see one another?

3. What role can Christians play in promoting reconciliation and mutual respect when social media often fuels outrage and division? How can we reflect Christ's love in our digital and face-to-face interactions?

4. Paul calls believers to prioritize relationships in Christ over judgment. What practical steps can you take to embody this in your daily interactions? What suggestions do you have for working towards unity in our church without compromising the truth?

3

Whom Would Jesus Eat With?

Hospitality and the Lord's Supper

SPENCER BOERSMA

"ONE EARLY, CLOUDY MORNING when I was forty-six," writes Sarah Miles, "I walked into a church, ate a piece of bread, took a sip of wine. A routine Sunday activity for tens of millions of Americans—except until that moment, I'd led a thoroughly secular life, at best indifferent to religion, more often appalled by its fundamentalist crusades. This was my first communion. It changed everything."[1] This is the beginning of Miles's spiritual memoir, an autobiography of sorts about how she, a person who grew up and had lived a completely irreligious life, one day, walking down the street in San Francisco, felt drawn into St. Gregory of Nyssa's Episcopal Church on a Sunday morning. This church practiced an innovative liturgy, where the sanctuary was organized in a circle around a central table, and the priests there invited anyone to come and partake of the Lord's Supper. Sarah Miles felt drawn to the table, and she describes the moment as an event of inexplicable spiritual epiphany. As she ate, she realized

1. Miles, *Take This Bread*, xiii.

25

for the first time in her life that God was with her. She was eating with God because God had invited her to God's table.

And with some awkward and tense moments, Miles informed her family and friends that she was now a Christian. She did not quite understand what it meant, but she knew she had been captivated by this reality and needed to pursue it. After this, she felt called to serve her community using her passion for food. Her memoir tells the story of how she opened up St. Gregory's Food Pantry, a free source of food for anyone who came, a pantry that came to feed thousands of the city's poor on a weekly basis. This ministry was an act that she saw as flowing from the reality of communion itself, one and the same. As God meets us in the meal of bread and wine, whether we are saints or sinners (or, more accurately, an awkward mixture of both), God meets our needs for forgiveness and love, and so, also, we meet each other in our differences; we meet in our needs for each other, for fellowship, food, provision, and care. This is the hospitality of the Lord's table: God's hospitality towards sinners, the church's hospitality towards those in need, those different than each other—a hospitality the church has often forgotten. This chapter seeks to recall churches to the practice modelled by Jesus himself—sometimes called open communion—as it seeks an open invitation for anyone to come and eat.

SETTING (THE THEOLOGY OF) THE OPEN TABLE

To be sure, communion (or the Eucharist) is the regular practice of covenanted disciples, done to remember and express thanksgiving for the sacrifice of Christ and hope in his coming. However, for many, it is a restricted practice, whether it is limited to baptized disciples, disciples baptized by immersion, or disciples baptized by immersion who are specific members of a particular denomination or church—various ways the table is policed in order for it to stay "pure." On the other hand, for many churches I have seen, communion is practiced by allowing anyone to come forward, leaving it up to their conscience, with no questions asked but very little reflection or rationale as to why. The table is not fenced purely out of convenience. Most churches, then, practice open communion without getting around to admitting it and, in doing so, fail to realize the gift and opportunity such a practice really is.

Very early in church history, the restricted form of communion became normative, and the meal and the remembrance were separated.[2] There were surely positive reasons for this, not least of which were the pressures of persecution, driving the church into a guarded secrecy, as well as the various abuses of the Love Feast. Some would point out that it has been the normative practice to restrict the table for most of church history (as early as the instructions in the Didache). However, to reflect on this vital church practice in the Free Church tradition, as a Baptist, is to say that if Christ is our ultimate rule, then Christ is the judge of all our traditions, no matter how old or predominant a tradition is. Thus, we must ask: "What is Jesus' pattern of communion?" Or, in Charles Sheldon-esque manner, simply, "Whom would Jesus eat with?"

Without asking this, there is this perennial tendency, as Jürgen Moltmann calls it, to turn "the Lord's Supper into the church's supper."[3] The open meal, too often, has become a closed ritual. However, dissenting Christians throughout church history have attempted recoveries and reappropriations in varieties of the open pattern. The most noteworthy of which, for this essay, are the ways some early Baptists—due to their awareness that salvation was much wider than their practices of baptism—kept the table open to those baptized differently.[4] Others include the Anabaptist communities who, striving to recover New Testament church patterns, practiced Love Feasts in various ways. Also, Methodists, in their devout evangelistic fervour, often opened communion to non-Christians, using the act of eating together as an invitation to "taste and see that the LORD is good" (Ps 34:8 NRSV). Meanwhile, social gospelers, in their desire to enact the kingdom of God, recognized

2. See Witherington, *Making a Meal*.
3. Moltmann, *Church in the Power*, 245.
4. See essays by Fiddes and Clarke.

that spoken good news is often empty if acts of service do not accompany it, and so were instrumental in forming meal ministries to feed the poor. These traditions I see as contributing strands to a holistic practice of open communion that is ecumenically minded just as much as it is potentially evangelistic, a practice that is just as much about fellowship as forgiveness, provision just as much as proclamation, service just as much as ceremony.

JESUS' PATTERN OF TABLE FELLOWSHIP

Communion is the meal God invites us to, and Jesus shows us paradigmatically whom he eats with leading up to the Last Supper: in the feeding of the five thousand, in eating with tax collectors and sinners, and, specifically, in eating with Zacchaeus. First, Jesus feeds the five thousand (Matt 14:13–21; Mark 6:30–44; Luke 9:10–17; John 6:1–14). As the story shows, the people are hungry, and Jesus simply has compassion for them. He could have shamed them for not being prepared. He could have decided who was really a disciple and who was not, who was a circumcised member of Israel or not. He could have created a system of criteria of who was deserving and who was actually a freeloader. But he didn't. Jesus simply has compassion for them.

Bread and fish are offered, and some have used that to say this is not the same as communion. However, if communion was a part of the Love Feast in some way, they were elements of a single meal. Catacomb paintings found in Rome depict early Christians conducting "agape" feasts; fish and bread are depicted in these paintings.

Fresco at a tomb in the Catacomb of Saints Marcellinus and Peter,
Via Labicana, Rome[5]

(Also, notice a woman is presiding and children are present at the
meal as well.) This suggests that early Christians certainly saw this
story as a paradigm for the meals they conducted.

The passages relating to feeding the five thousand go out of
the way to use the language that Jesus thanked God, "blessed and
broke" the bread. The words used here are similar to those of Jesus during the Last Supper: blessing and breaking. Jesus is doing
something here that is like what he does there. Jesus is establishing
a pattern with whom he chooses to eat.

The second story is about Jesus calling Matthew and then eating with sinners and tax collectors (Matt 9:9–13). The treasurer of
First Baptist of Sudbury, Ontario (where I pastored for five years),
was a retired accountant for the CRA, and we would always joke,
"See, God even loves tax collectors like Carl!" (And he would joke
back, "But what has the Bible got against tax collectors? It's an honest profession!") But, of course, tax collecting had a different role

5. Unknown author, retrieved from https://en.wikipedia.org/wiki/Agape_
feast#/media/File:Agape_feast_03.jpg. Public domain.

in the Roman Empire. The Roman occupation hired these people to get money from others to pay for the occupation. These individuals were considered traitors to their people and were often thugs. Jesus makes a point of calling a tax collector to be his disciple. Jesus is making a statement: it does not matter who you are; Jesus' way of new life, his kingdom, is for you. This blows Matthew away, and it seems that he and a bunch of his friends come to dinner that night and eat with Jesus. The story makes a point of saying that there are tax collectors and known sinners but also disciples at the meal. Both are invited, and Jesus eats with both.

Eating for a Jew was something deeply religious. Every meal was a religious feast in miniature. Jews could not eat with non-Jews. One was considered holy; the other was not. Jesus, however, ignores this. In fact, he transgresses this, which enrages the religious leaders who are watching. Jesus responds to them with words that the church, frankly, has struggled to live out for two thousand years, echoing the prophet Hosea: "Those who are well have no need of a physician, but those who are sick. Go and learn what this means, 'I desire mercy, not sacrifice.' For I have come to call not the righteous but sinners" (Matt 9:12–13 NRSV; see Hos 6:6).

The third story follows in this vein. Jesus eats with the tax collector, Zacchaeus (Luke 19:1–10). Again, tax collectors were viewed as scum, yet this particular person, when he hears that Jesus is coming, due to his short stature, climbs a tree in order to see Jesus. Jesus calls to him to eat with him and, again, the religious leaders are upset. Zacchaeus is so moved that he pledges to give half of his possessions to the poor and repay those he has cheated fourfold. Jesus changes Zacchaeus's life by eating with him, reconciling him back into the family of God. He is redeemed through the table meal, not apart from it.

Unsurprisingly, when we look at the story of the Last Supper, the passage that institutes communion for the first time, we see Jesus eating in a manner consistent with all the other meals he shared. We see him going out of his way to point out that he knows the disciples he is eating with—especially Judas and Peter—will betray, deny, and desert him (Mark 14:12–31; Matt 26:17–35; Luke

30

22:7–34). Jesus eats with them anyway. Jesus says to them: this is my body broken, and this is my blood poured out as a new covenant—a new understanding of God's relationship—poured out for the forgiveness of sins. If that is the occasion of the new covenant, it would seem odd that communion should be marked by criteria of worthiness, reserved for those who meet that standard.

While the disciples betrayed and deserted Jesus, the religious leaders accused the Messiah of blasphemy, the Romans tortured Jesus, and the people jeered and mocked, Jesus used this moment to show us what kind of God he truly is. God chose to step into our hate to bring us his love. God chose to step into our darkness to bring his light. When we embraced sin, God bore our death and, in exchange, gave us his life. When humanity turned from God, God in Christ resolved to be with us. So, communion draws us into this truth of our faith, this mystery beyond our understanding: God loves us so much that God gave of his very self; God loves us with his very body and blood. This is the reality—this body, this blood—that we are called to a "participation" (Gk: *koinonia*) in taking the bread and wine (1 Cor 10:15–17).

LIVING THE TABLE'S HOSPITALITY

We must recognize that communion is the church's mission in miniature: God calls us to be with others as God is with us. This begins with eating together and realizing the full breadth of God's family, encountering each other's differences in the space of the table's reconciling unity. Communion is to eat with each other as an encounter with God. Communion is the sign that the infinitely perfect God has chosen to be one with finite, sinful humanity. In crossing this divide, communion prompts us to encounter others different than ourselves, seeing ourselves in and through others.

Despite communion being a sign that God chooses to be with sinners, many have worried that to open up communion would be to open the church up to the possibility of partaking in an "unworthy manner" after the warnings of Paul in 1 Cor 11:17–33 (NRSV). However, the "unworthy manner" (v. 27) was not that sinners were taking communion but the very manner of communion itself, where there were "divisions" in the body (v. 18): the rich were gobbling up the food before the poor could arrive and be fed. The "unworthy manner" is any practice of communion that visibly communicates to others the sense that they are of lesser worth in God's family.

While pastoring, I constantly encountered people who didn't take communion because they did not feel worthy, worried they would drink judgment upon themselves. My response to that is simply that if you feel unworthy of coming to God's table, that is precisely why God is inviting you with open arms. We do not stay away from God's presence to make ourselves better; it is the presence of God that invites us in and heals us. Communion is a sign that God invites us to his table as undeserving sinners to nourish us with grace.

It may be that the Love Feast was regulated and eventually discontinued because it was being done in its own "unworthy manner." Early church documents called for oversight of the Love Feast.[6] Perhaps some early Christians used it to celebrate too frivolously, which was not a good witness to the gospel. However, if in the early church the excesses of the Love Feasts became a scandal to the gospel, perhaps today it is the opposite: today's scandal is that communion is so over ritualized, routine, even joyless.

Communion teaches us that we must share—share with the generosity God has with us, share our lives with each other as God gives the gift of God's very self, and thus, share in such a way that sees our mutual struggle for flourishing not as a competition against one another but rather a striving that lifts each other up together. Sadly, the church has capitulated to the worldly sense of individuality and autonomy, an egocentrism that turns communities into fragmented, warring tribes. Yet, if we contemplate the reality of communion, the miracles that were Jesus' life, death, and resurrection prompt us, transform us, to live this reality in all kinds of beautiful yet mundane ways.

6 E.g., Ignatius, *To the Smyrnaeans.*

There is a Jewish story called *Bone Button Borscht* by Aubrey Davis. It is the whimsical story of a mysterious beggar—perhaps an angel in disguise—who comes to a gloomy town that has forgotten how to share. He goes door to door requesting hospitality, each time getting denied. He finally comes to a synagogue where even the caretaker (called a shamas) is cold to him. The beggar, however, promises he will work a miracle and produce the most wonderful soup (or borscht) if only the shamas would give him just an old bone button. Finally, out of intrigue, the shamas, who has no buttons, pleads with his neighbour, a tailor, for a spare. Intrigued over the promise of a miracle, the neighbour donates the button. Another neighbour hears and, again, out of intrigue, donates a pot. Another donates a spoon. Soon, the whole town gathers around the beggar, who is stirring a pot of hot water. He sips the soup and says, "This soup is wonderful, but you know what would make it better? Some potatoes." Eagerly, a villager donates some potatoes. Another donates cabbage. Another gets spices. Another says, "Why don't I get some bread? It's not every day we get to eat a miracle!" Still another decides to break out wine. Another decides, "You know what would go well with this meal? Music." Soon, a joyous feast comes together, and everyone agrees that the soup is the most delightful soup everyone has ever tasted. It easily feeds the whole town with some to spare. After the feast, the beggar says he must go, but the villagers plead with him to give them more buttons so that they can keep making this wonderful soup. So, he produces a handful of buttons and disappears. The villagers keep making the soup, but after the buttons run out, they catch on to the fact that they really do not need buttons at all.[7]

With his "miracle," the beggar causes a paradigm shift that inspires the village to keep living the "miracle" out. Similarly, Jesus' kingdom signs direct us back on the way of the kingdom, living as pointers to it, living as signs of its presence now, despite living in a world of sin, domination, and fragmentation. The meal was not merely a ritual. It performed the kingdom despite not being

7. Davis, *Bone Button Borscht*, 8.

33

"miraculous" in the way Jesus' initial signs were. Hospitality, however, can be those small acts that grow into miracles.

The meal is, then, so much more than just a meal. In this regard, as R. Alan Streett notes, the communion banquets for the early church were visible and embodied witnesses against the oppression of the empire.[8] The Roman Empire sustained itself on the hierarchal divides of men over women, Roman citizens over subjects, and slave owners over slaves. Yet, the Christian practice of communion brought all together in a banquet that transgressed these boundaries in equalizing and dignifying ways (e.g., Luke 14:13–14). By eating in this manner, people can realize that true riches are found in sharing, not hoarding. They can realize that true security is found in inclusion, not exclusion. They can realize that true status is found in mercy, not superiority. Paul reminds us, "Because there is one bread, we who are many are one body, for we all partake of the one bread" (1 Cor 10:17 NRSV). M. Shawn Copeland writes:

> We know in our bodies that eating the bread and drinking the wine involves something much deeper and far more extensive than consuming elements of the ritual meal. Eucharistic solidarity is a virtue, a practice of cognitive and bodily commitments oriented to meet the social consequences of Eucharist. We women and men strive to become what we have received and to do what we are being made.[9]

Communion is not something we merely take. It is something we live and become with others as God is bringing us together.

Ironically, we can fixate so much on the bread and the wine that we forget this. One time, I was reminded of this when leading communion. That Sunday, a family who had not come to church in a long time visited the church. It was a single mother with three children, one with autism. She was invited to church by the worship leader, who taught her children music lessons. She sheepishly showed up late and sat at the back. During communion, her son got

8. Streett, *Subversive Meals*.
9. Copeland, *Enfleshing Freedom*, 132.

34

overwhelmed and started running around the church. Then he ran up to me and ran off with the communion cup. I was flabbergasted, but then it occurred to me that God was up to something much more important than that cup. I took a moment to say that having this child with us, this particular Sunday, might be the Spirit's way of teaching us about the meaning of communion if we were willing to see it. While the mother was still embarrassed, some mothers in the congregation came around her, sat with her, and let her know it was all right. This was communion. If communion does not propel us to see others, see their differences and struggles, draw close to them, mourn with those who mourn, and rejoice with those who rejoice (Rom 12:15), we are not truly practicing communion. Communion is a meal in hope, taken in expectation and anticipation, like the Passover feast before the liberation of the Exodus, like the Last Supper before the resurrection. Paul reminds us, "For as often as you eat this bread and drink the cup, you proclaim the Lord's death until he comes" (1 Cor 11:26 NRSV). The prophet Isaiah envisions what that final, eternal feast will one day be like when God will "wipe away the tears from all faces" and "swallow up death forever" (Isa 25:6–9 NRSV). And so, we remember the God who meets with us in the meal, anticipating that day when God's presence will be perfect in all and through all.

While in my doctoral studies, I coordinated a soup kitchen in downtown Toronto. The people who came were often the sort of people churches didn't want around. It was here that I really understood who "the poor" were. Poverty finally had a face, and I realized just how badly we scapegoat the poor as lazy or dangerous. We do not want to face the fact that many of us are one tragedy away from poverty. We do not want to face the fact that poverty is a complicated condition involving abuse, health, accessibility, and more—things that require a community response if we are really going to uphold the dignity we believe God has placed in every person.

Many who came for food at the soup kitchen had been abused by different churches. Many did not know what to believe, but since they knew I was in seminary and we met in the basement of a church, this meal program, the Gathering Spot, became for many their church, and they called me their pastor. And so, every Tuesday night, I found myself the unofficial pastor of an unofficial church of a flock of misfit sheep. Communion was often shared at the Gathering Spot, inviting the needy of the community—sometimes those experiencing homelessness or individuals strung out from their addictions—to come and partake. One of my favourite sayings about evangelism is that "sharing the gospel is just one beggar telling another beggar where to find bread." As I have come to realize, quite literally, how could this not include for the marginalized the very bread broken as God's promise of love towards sinners?

The cup used in communion at the Gathering Spot, which was given to me as a gift after the program closed down. It now proudly sits on my office shelf.

My teammate was a saintly older Dutch lady named Marijke. She was a lady full of the Spirit. She used to work in real estate but quit her job because she was told to sell nice properties only to White people to keep rich neighbourhoods prestigious. As she told me, "That was not the way of my Jesus," and so she quit. Being a good Dutch lady, she would penny-pinch, and we could make a few dollars and obtain donations to feed dozens: thirty to fifty people every Tuesday. And she would sing and pray as she cooked.

Some nights, we ran out of food, but I remember one time when we had more guests than usual, and only a little bit was left in the pot. I remember seeing it and thinking we didn't have enough—two or three bowls at best. But she kept scooping and praying, and I kept serving it out, another and another and another, until everyone was fed and full. I thought there was simply no way that the amount left was enough to feed that many people, but Marijke just smiled and kept singing. Serving in a soup kitchen taught me the deeper meaning of communion. To eat and drink, to remember and hope, are not merely rituals of a past event but rhythms for seeing moments of resurrection right now.

When I began pastoring First Baptist Church of Sudbury, I tried to integrate into our worship both word and deed, particularly for those less fortunate in our community. Often, I or another church member would pick people up for church and, if they were in need, there were always containers of food that families brought in and stored in the church's refrigerator. On communion Sundays, we invited the children to bring up food bank donations, placing them on the communion table as part of the communion act, alongside the bread and the wine. Some folks would ask for a ride to church because it was the end of the month and they knew there was food for them there. And so, every communion Sunday, I invoked these precious words from the Baptist Union of Great Britain's *Gathering for Worship*:

> Come to this table, not because you must but because you may,
>
> not because you are strong, but because you are weak.

Come, not because any goodness of your own gives you
a right to come,

but because you need mercy and help.

Come, because you love the Lord a little and would like
to love him more.

Come, because he loved you and gave himself for you.

Come and meet the risen Christ, for we are his Body.[10]

CONCLUSION: WHOM WILL WE WELCOME?

I learned in these experiences that the medium is the message, so
communion must be as open as the gospel it proclaims. The open
pattern of the Lord's Supper, displayed in the messianic feasts that
Jesus enacted, is something we are invited to emulate.

Christ welcomes us to his table. Who is welcome at ours?
Atlantic Canada has seen an influx of immigration in historic
numbers, which many have said is vital to our economic future.
Let me suggest that these movements are vital to our spiritual
future as well. The Spirit of Christ has been faithful in the history of the Atlantic, but we must also realize that the Spirit is
blowing with new winds. This means, in part, the Spirit "comes
from away": the Spirit's ways are free, diverse, messy, surprising,
uncontrollable, and, if we welcome them, exciting, prophetic, re-
freshing, and revitalizing. Will the Spirit be accepted, or will the
Spirit never truly be seen as "one of us"?

Christians in the Atlantic, particularly Baptists, are becoming
aware that our neighbourhoods and churches are no longer just
"us." Indeed, there have always been the "others," those on the margins of our communities. Will we police our fellowship—symbol-
ized fundamentally in the communion table—in reaction to this
diversity, attempting to hold onto a past that is increasingly not our
present and future? Will the Lord's table reflect our churchly colo-
nizations, or will it reflect Christ's coming kingdom? It is simple:
Whom would Jesus eat with? Whom will we eat with? Will we live

10. Baptist Union, *Gathering for Worship*, 14.

38

Christ's hospitality—hospitality that is not shallow inclusiveness or lip-service friendliness, but the kind that brings out the best of East Coast culture: the sharing of life and laughter, good food and good conversation, and caring for one another like we are truly family? The body of Christ is so much bigger than just us. This body has faces very different than our own and involves people from different places than here, who, in fact, are showing up here in our congregational bodies. Will we welcome Christ in them?

SUGGESTIONS FOR FURTHER READING

Baptist Union of Great Britain, The. *Gathering for Worship: Patterns and Prayers for the Community of Disciples*, edited by Christopher Ellis and Myra Blyth. Norwich: Canterbury, 2005.

Clarke, Anthony. "A Feast for All? Reflecting on Open Communion for the Contemporary Church." In *Baptist Sacramentalism 2*, edited by Anthony R. Cross and Philip E. Thompson, 92–116. Studies in Baptist History and Thought. Eugene, OR: Wipf and Stock, 2009.

Copeland, M. Shawn. *Enfleshing Freedom: Body, Race, and Being*. 2nd ed. Minneapolis: Fortress, 2023.

Fiddes, Paul S. *Tracks and Traces: Baptist Identity in Church and Theology*. Eugene: Wipf and Stock, 2007. Studies in Baptist History and Thought. See ch. 8, "The Church as Eucharistic Community: A Baptist Contribution," in particular.

Miles, Sarah. *Take This Bread: A Radical Conversion*. New York: Ballantine, 2007.

Moltmann, Jürgen. *The Church in the Power of the Spirit: A Contribution to Messianic Ecclesiology*. Translated by Margaret Kohl. Minneapolis: Fortress, 1993.

Streett, R. Alan. *Subversive Meals: An Analysis of the Lord's Supper Under Roman Dominations During the First Century*. Eugene, OR: Wipf and Stock, 2013.

Witherington, Ben, III. *Making a Meal of It: Rethinking the Theology of the Lord's Supper*. Waco: Baylor University Press, 2007. An excellent book from a Wesleyan perspective that goes through the major New Testament passages and early history of the communion meal.

BIBLIOGRAPHY

Baptist Union of Great Britain, The. *Gathering for Worship: Patterns and Prayers for the Community of Disciples*, edited by Christopher Ellis and Myra Blyth. Norwich: Canterbury, 2005.

Copeland, M. Shawn. *Enfleshing Freedom: Body, Race, and Being*. 2nd ed. Minneapolis: Fortress, 2023.

Davis, Aubrey. *Bone Button Borscht*. Toronto: Kids Can, 1995.

Miles, Sarah. *Take This Bread: A Radical Conversion*. New York: Ballantine, 2007.

Moltmann, Jürgen. *The Church in the Power of the Spirit: A Contribution to Messianic Ecclesiology*. Translated by Margaret Kohl. Minneapolis: Fortress, 1993.

DISCUSSION QUESTIONS

1. What has been the practice of communion at your church? Who partakes? How is this communicated, if at all?

2. Reflect on a time when you found taking communion was particularly meaningful. What was significant about that moment?

3. How can the practices of the Lord's Supper be integrated with what the church does in its fellowship and ministry?

4

A Warm Welcome or a Closed Door?

Transforming the Myths of East Coast Hospitality

ANNA ROBBINS[1]

IN 2014, THE PROVINCIAL government commissioned the Nova Scotia Commission on Building our Economy to compile what has become known as the Ivany report, named after Ray Ivany, chair of the commission. *Now or Never: An Urgent Call to Action for Nova Scotians* set goals to revive the economy and set this East Coast province on a new trajectory for success.[2] One of the most important observations in the report was that immigration and empowerment of racialized populations are essential to innovation and entrepreneurship in Atlantic Canada. At the same time, although Atlantic Canada is most successful when it is hospitable

1. This article is drawn from the content of my Hayward Lectures delivered at ADC in 2021. I enjoyed an engaging collaboration with AI assistance, which supported the integration and refinement of this work.

2. See Nova Scotia Commission, *Now or Never*.

to newcomers and empowering diverse communities, there has been suspicion of outsiders taking jobs and accruing advantages that make Nova Scotians wary of showing too much hospitality to newcomers. Newcomers and racialized communities have not always found it easy to flourish on the East Coast of Canada. To what can we attribute such a view, and what role do the churches have to play when it comes to offering authentic hospitality from a place of humble confidence as Atlantic Canadians? Is it possible that Christians could contribute to the well-being of society by simply practicing their basic call to hospitality?

Hospitality is perceived as a deeply rooted value in East Coast culture, often associated with open doors, hearty meals, and a sense of belonging. The reality of such hospitality becomes more complex when placed in historical context. While settler people were welcomed to this land through the generosity and support of Indigenous communities, the return welcome often narrowed to serve colonial interests and privilege selected identities. In more recent times, culture has birthed a pervasive East Coast nostalgia—a longing for a past that is often romanticized and selectively remembered. But selling ourselves a nostalgic vision of hospitality does not actually make us hospitable. While nostalgia can offer comfort and a sense of shared identity, it can also act as a barrier to genuine hospitality, especially when it fosters exclusion or inhibits our active welcome of new Canadians to our region, our neighbourhoods, and our churches.

In this chapter we will explore how nostalgia shapes East Coast identity and the practice of hospitality. Drawing on theological insights and cultural analysis, we will examine how nostalgia can work against genuine hospitality and propose pathways for transforming nostalgia into a tool for inclusive and forward-looking welcome. It is possible that within our critique of nostalgic remembrance, we may find seeds of hope to renew our East Coast culture as a unique place of radical hospitality and true belonging in an often lonely and isolating world.

UNDERSTANDING NOSTALGIA
AND ITS THEOLOGICAL IMPLICATIONS

Nostalgia, derived from the Greek roots *nostos* (home) and *algia* (pain), originally described the homesickness experienced by displaced individuals. This term was first coined by Swiss physician Johannes Hofer in the seventeenth century to describe the profound yearning for home that afflicted soldiers serving far from their native land. Hofer noted that nostalgia manifested not only emotionally but physically, with symptoms such as melancholy, loss of appetite, and even heart palpitations. The cure for such a malady was a return home.[3]

By the eighteenth and nineteenth centuries, nostalgia's definition broadened. It was no longer seen as a specific medical condition but as a cultural and emotional phenomenon tied to the human experience of time and memory. Romantic poets such as Wordsworth explored nostalgia as a deep connection to one's past, often framing it as a longing for innocence, simplicity, or unity with nature. This era laid the foundation for understanding nostalgia as both a personal and collective experience—a way of shaping identity by remembering the past.

In the twentieth century, the rise of industrialization, mass migration, and rapid societal change gave nostalgia a new cultural significance. People began to associate it with the loss of tradition and stability. Sociologists identified nostalgia as a way to cope with dislocation and uncertainty. Nostalgia became both a comfort and a critique, offering a refuge from the alienation of modernity while subtly resisting the inevitability of change.

Today, nostalgia has become culturally pervasive, amplified by digital technology and consumer culture. Social media platforms help us to curate our present activities as future memories, creating our future nostalgic moments. Commercial industries commodify nostalgia, repackaging childhood toys, retro fashions, and classic TV shows to market a sense of familiarity and comfort. This cultural ubiquity of nostalgia underscores its dual

---

3. Hofer, "Medical Dissertation on Nostalgia," 381.

nature: while it can foster connection and continuity, it can also distort history, prioritize idealized memories over complex truths, and hinder progress.

From a theological perspective, nostalgia can mirror the human longing for God and ultimate belonging. As C. S. Lewis described in many of his writings, this yearning—what he termed *Sehnsucht* or "joy"—is an inconsolable desire for something beyond this world. Lewis argued that nostalgia, when rightly directed, reflects humanity's deeper hunger for the divine. However, nostalgia can also be misdirected. It can become an idolatry of the past, where people seek fulfillment in recreating lost moments or imagined glory rather than embracing the transformative work of God in the present and future. This tension makes nostalgia a powerful yet ambivalent force in both personal spirituality and communal life.

There is something inherent in all of us to long for home, or at least some version of it. Theologically speaking, home is not something we build or protect; it is a gift. We are created for our home with God. But we seek it in many other places, striving to be satisfied in ever-empty experiences and venues, and never finding fulfillment. The Christian story reveals a God who makes God's home with humanity, dwelling among us to reconcile and renew. In this sense, hospitality is not an obligation imposed but a reflection of divine generosity. When we understand home as a gift from God, our own rootedness in place becomes a source of strength for extending that welcome to others. Ultimately, our homes are not ours but God's, and the hospitality we extend reflects the welcome we have already received in Christ.

NOSTALGIA ON CANADA'S EAST COAST: A CULTURAL LENS

Most East Coast people hold a strong sense of home. Those who go away for school or work very often return "home" later in life, drawn by the values and identity tied to place. Outsiders, too, are often captivated by the sense of home East Coasters exude, and home and family remain strong traditional values in the region. While this rootedness can lend itself to exclusivity, it also holds the seedbed for authentic hospitality. When East Coasters find their identity in home secure, they may discover a greater capacity for vulnerability as hosts—a readiness to extend the welcome that creates a sense of home for others.

At the same time, East Coast history reveals that many physical homesteads were built on the displacement and homelessness of others. The expulsion of the Acadians, the dispossession of Indigenous lands, and the systemic marginalization of African Nova Scotians remind us that the homes cherished by some came at the cost of others losing theirs. This legacy challenges us to rethink the meaning of home and hospitality, especially in a world where loneliness is pervasive, and many have been forced from their homes by global conflict or economic hardship. True hospitality invites us to create spaces where others can find belonging. Can East Coasters say with integrity, "This is home—welcome to your home too"?

East Coast identity is deeply intertwined with its history and geography. This is true everywhere in Atlantic Canada, perhaps especially so in Nova Scotia. The province's branding as a picturesque haven—evoked in images of lighthouses, fishing villages, and Celtic traditions—relies heavily on nostalgia. This idealization, while charming, often masks a more complex and uncomfortable history.

In their book *In the Province of History*, Ian McKay and Robin Bates critique Nova Scotia's "therapeutic nostalgia," which romanticizes the past while avoiding critical reflection on historical injustices. This nostalgia was evident in past tourism campaigns that celebrated colonial and Celtic heritage while sidelining other more diverse stories. Significant historical events, including expulsion, dispossession, and marginalization, were ignored or downplayed in favour of a more idyllic narrative. The horrific expulsion of the Acadians became the romanticized story of Evangeline, marketing the province as an attractive and welcoming tourist destination.

McKay and Bates argue that this curated image of the past supports a province-as-museum concept, where Nova Scotia was not so much a place to live as a destination to visit. This version of history, popularized in the twentieth century, emphasized colonial settlement, romanticized rural life, and reified Celtic traditions, all while ignoring the systemic inequities that defined the region. McKay and Bates highlight how the Scottish tartan myth was constructed as a unifying symbol of identity, even as it erased diverse experiences and histories. Anyone could belong, so long as they adopted a tartan to wear and pretended to be Scottish. But this myth draws lines between who really is at home here and who is not.[4]

The nostalgic framing of identity in Nova Scotia extends beyond physical spaces to cultural practices. Festivals, for instance, often center around reenactments or celebrations of a Celtic or colonial past, implicitly suggesting that these histories define what it means to be Nova Scotian. Many of the historical details portrayed defy verification. Yet, these narratives frequently define belonging, and exclude the experiences and contributions of non-European communities. The collective memory promoted through these events emphasizes unity, but it is a unity that comes at the expense of diversity.

This cultural nostalgia creates a paradox: while East Coasters bask in a historical reputation for extending hospitality, the nostalgic framing of identity can foster exclusion. It can divide *insiders* from *outsiders* and privilege an imagined "home" over the reality of diverse, contemporary communities. The phrase "come from away," often applied to newcomers even after many years of settlement, illustrates how deeply ingrained this sense of belonging is—and how difficult it is to break into the imagined *insider* community.

Churches in the region are not immune to this trend. Many church communities focus on preserving a nostalgic image of themselves—be it in architectural styles, music, or events—at the expense of engaging with contemporary challenges. While these practices can create a sense of a stable home, they also risk alienating those who feel excluded from these traditions,

4. McKay and Bates, *In the Province*, 275.

particularly younger generations and those from different cultural backgrounds. Yet, while some churches seek to preserve a nostalgic vision of the past, they find themselves increasingly isolated in a culture that has rapidly transformed around them.

In sum, nostalgia provides an insufficient basis for authentic hospitality. The nostalgic lens through which some East Coast Canadians view their history and identity, while comforting, often serves as a barrier to true hospitality. By clinging to a romanticized past, communities risk perpetuating exclusion and missing the opportunity to embrace the richness of a diverse and dynamic present.

RESTORATIONIST NOSTALGIA: RETREATING TO THE PAST IN THE FACE OF PROGRESS

Restorationist nostalgia takes this dynamic a step further by attempting to reclaim and reestablish an imagined and idealized past. While often appealing as a response to societal change, restorationist nostalgia represents a new polarizing, political nationalism. Instead of fostering a shared understanding of community, it frequently leans into power and control, privileging the perspectives of a select few. It feeds on suspicion of the outsider and the misunderstood. It is highly protective of its version of home. Such polarization is particularly impactful among Christians, where restorationist nostalgia can amplify divisions rather than build bridges of understanding and inclusivity.

Restorationist nostalgia represents a longing not simply to remember the past but also to recreate it as a guide for the future. Unlike reflective nostalgia, which critically engages with memories, restorationist nostalgia idealizes the past and seeks to recast it in the present—often without acknowledging its complexities or failings. In the face of modern challenges and rapid cultural shifts, restorationist nostalgia provides a perceived anchor of stability. Yet, this anchor can prevent communities from moving forward with honesty and adaptability.

This form of nostalgia is evident in many aspects of East Coast culture. Festivals, heritage districts, and even church practices often aim to replicate a romanticized version of the past. These efforts can create a comforting sense of continuity but risk excluding those whose experiences and identities were marginalized in the historical narratives being celebrated. For example, the "good old days" often celebrated in these reenactments ignore the systemic injustices faced by Mi'kmaq communities, African Nova Scotians, and others who were excluded or harmed during these so-called golden eras.

Restorationist nostalgia often emerges in response to perceived threats to cultural identity. The rapid pace of globalization, immigration, and technological progress can make communities feel unmoored. In this context, nostalgia becomes a rallying cry for preservation—a way to resist change and maintain (or regain) a sense of control. However, this resistance often relies on selective memory, erasing uncomfortable truths about the past. It can also lead to exclusionary practices, where only those who fit the idealized image of the community are fully welcomed.

From a theological perspective, restorationist nostalgia can hinder the church's mission by focusing on institutional survival rather than spiritual transformation. Churches that cling to outdated practices and resist necessary adaptations risk becoming irrelevant to contemporary communities. Moreover, restorationist nostalgia can blind churches to the ways God is at work in the present, calling them to new forms of ministry and witness.

The danger of restorationist nostalgia lies in its promise of a return to "better times" that never truly existed. The Christian call is not to recreate an idealized past but to live faithfully in the present, responding to the needs of the world as it is. For East Coast communities, this means moving beyond restorationist nostalgia to embrace a more dynamic and inclusive vision of hospitality—one that acknowledges the past without being constrained by it.

AUTHENTIC HOSPITALITY
AS VULNERABILITY AT HOME

When we think about hospitality, we are called to embrace the vulnerability of truth telling. Authentic hospitality calls us to move beyond the comfort of nostalgic narratives and confront the realities of our history and our present. Past and present privilege demands honesty about the exclusions and injustices that may underlie the stories we tell about ourselves as East Coast settler people. Perhaps the narrative of East Coast hospitality, celebrated as generous and warm, is itself shaped more by nostalgia than reality. This kind of vulnerability requires us to reconsider our identity, as those who have participated in a story of racism and exclusion while basking in nostalgic ideals. It also calls us to commit to a deeper, more radical practice of welcome, rather than retreat into an isolationist, revisionist ideal.

The history of East Coast settlers underscores the need for truth telling. Early relationships between settlers and the Mi'kmaq people were marked by peace and friendship treaties, which demonstrated the hospitality and generosity of the Mi'kmaq. They shared resources, knowledge, and welcome, enabling settlers to survive in a harsh environment. However, these acts of hospitality were often met with betrayal, as settlers violated the treaties, displaced Indigenous communities, and claimed the land as their own. This tragic history reveals that the celebrated narrative of East Coast hospitality often ignores the harm done to those who first extended welcome. By taking history seriously, we are called to reflect on whether our reputation for hospitality is misplaced and to reimagine it through honesty and justice. Racism and exclusion are yet a reality in many churches, often leaving the Christian practice of authentic hospitality in the dust.

In more recent years, we have perhaps also failed to notice our retreat into our homes and away from community. Our tables are very often filled with our family and closest friends—people who look and think like "us." We imagine the eschatological future as the banquet table in heaven, where our family gathers and Mother calls us in for supper. That nostalgic vision perhaps prevents us from viewing the eschatological banquet table with Jesus' eyes. The Lord's table is filled with those gathered from the highways and byways, who do not look or talk like we do. *This* is our home and our family. The eschatological table is so much more than our family dinner table projected into heaven. And the unity it portrays begins this side of glory.

Owning the facts of our history enables descendants of historical settlers—and others—to repent of our abuse and neglect of hospitality in the past, and seek an attitude of humble reconciliation with everyone who walks together in the beauty of East Coast land. Telling the stories truthfully and well also invites new Canadians into this journey of reconciliation as they find their place here.

CHALLENGES TO AUTHENTIC EAST COAST HOSPITALITY

To summarize, these are the real and continuing challenges that keep our Christian communities from demonstrating authentic hospitality:

Exclusion Through Nostalgia

Nostalgia often establishes boundaries that exclude those who do not fit into the romanticized narrative of the past. For example, newcomers to Nova Scotia—whether immigrants, refugees, or interprovincial migrants—may encounter subtle resistance as they are labeled "from away." This phrase, while seemingly harmless, reinforces an "us versus them" mindset, undermining the inclusivity that true hospitality requires.

Neglecting Justice

The selective memory of nostalgia can prevent communities from acknowledging and addressing historical injustices. Churches, for instance, may celebrate their role as community centers while neglecting to confront past complicity in segregation or colonialism. This lack of critical reflection stifles moral agency, reducing the church's ability to act as a transformative moral witness in our communities.

Comfort over Challenge

Nostalgia can lead to an overemphasis on comfort, prioritizing familiar rituals and traditions over the disruptive and often uncomfortable demands of godly hospitality. In protecting our time and limiting home to a few close friends and family, communities risk prioritizing self-preservation over sacrificial welcome.

REIMAGINING HOSPITALITY AS A THEOLOGICAL PRACTICE

Hospitality is central to the Christian faith, rooted in the biblical narrative of God making a home with humanity. From the hospitality of Abraham to the parable of the good Samaritan, Scripture calls believers to extend welcome beyond their immediate circles. In the incarnation, God's ultimate act of hospitality, Jesus dwelt among us, breaking down barriers of exclusion and reorienting the concept of home.

Our nostalgia for an imagined home often prevents us from practicing authentic and vulnerable hospitality. By clinging to an idealized version of home—one that reflects only our comforts, traditions, and preferences—we create boundaries that exclude those who do not fit into this nostalgic narrative. This version of home becomes static, a place of preservation rather than transformation. In striving to make our homes—or even our churches—reflect these nostalgic ideals, we risk distorting God's vision for home. Too often, we attempt to make God's home reflect our own rather than allowing our homes to be reshaped by the expansive and inclusive hospitality of God. This reversal stifles vulnerability, the essential element of true hospitality, and reinforces an "us versus them" mindset that hinders our ability to extend welcome to others—and to receive hospitality from neighbours and strangers. Yet the welcome of another can be truly transformative.

Hospitality is therefore not about guarding what we consider "ours," but about participating in the generosity of God, who has already opened his home to us. Rather, he left his home to make our place his dwelling. He has made his home among us. This theological insight radically shifts the focus of hospitality from nostalgia-driven exclusion to forward-looking inclusivity. When East Coasters say, "Welcome home," they echo the divine invitation extended to all humanity. This is especially poignant in a world rife with displacement and loneliness, where many are searching for a place to belong.

In this light, the church becomes a foretaste of the eschatological banquet—the eternal home God is preparing for all people. This vision transcends earthly nostalgia and reimagines home not as a static place, but as a dynamic relationship defined by mutual care, shared resources, and unconditional welcome. By embodying this radical hospitality, East Coast churches can point their communities toward a more authentic understanding of home—not as something we build or own, but as something we receive and share because of God's grace.

A PATH FORWARD:
TRANSFORMING NOSTALGIA FOR HOSPITALITY

A decade after the Ivany report, the call for immigration and the empowerment of racialized communities remains crucial to our well-being as community. While progress has been made, there is still work to be done. Churches, as communities rooted in a theology of hospitality, have a unique opportunity to contribute to this societal transformation.

Some East Coast churches are already pointing the way forward, offering hopeful examples of how hospitality can foster inclusivity and address historical injustices. These represent a hopeful trajectory that we can continue to engage as we undertake the following practices.

Embrace Reflective Nostalgia

Rather than seeking to recreate an idealized past, communities can use nostalgia as a tool for gratitude and reflection. For example, some churches have embraced intercultural community by including the wide range of cultures present in their cities and towns in fellowship and leadership. This demonstrates that reflective nostalgia can inspire communities to move beyond their comfort zones to build new, dynamic relationships.

Reimagine Church Spaces

Churches on the East Coast can rethink how their physical and social spaces are used. Instead of preserving buildings as monuments to the past, they can become centers for community engagement, welcoming newcomers, and addressing social needs. Some declining churches, for instance, have given over their facilities to newer and younger congregations, often of different cultural backgrounds, reflecting the biblical principle of sharing resources and space for the common good.

Cultivate Moral Courage

Hospitality requires the courage to confront uncomfortable truths. Many East Coast churches have excelled in welcoming large numbers of Syrian refugees as new Canadians, providing housing, language support, and pathways to inclusion. These efforts embody moral courage and demonstrate the church's capacity to act as a transformative moral witness.

Extend the Table

Godly hospitality calls for an ever-expanding table where all are welcome. Some churches have returned to the call for Christians to offer a welcome to everyone by sharing meals in homes and communities as a tangible expression of grace and hospitality. These acts remind us that the table is not just a metaphor but a lived reality that brings people together, breaking down the barriers between *insiders* and *outsiders*.

Celebrate the Vulnerability in "Home"

To be truly hospitable, communities must embrace vulnerability. When we open our homes and our churches to others, we acknowledge that home is a shared and sacred space rather than something exclusively ours. East Coasters, with their deep connection to home, have the potential to model this kind of openness, creating environments where everyone—long-time residents and newcomers alike—can find a place to belong.

CONCLUSION: NOSTALGIA REDEEMED

Ten years after the Ivany report, progress has been made, but its goals remain partially unfulfilled. Nova Scotia still struggles with the tension between its need for immigration and the empowerment of racialized communities, and its lingering suspicion of outsiders. Yet, the church has an opportunity to lead the way in redeeming the past and reimagining the future.

Nostalgia, when redeemed, can inspire hope and action rather than exclusion and complacency. For East Coast Canadians, this means transforming cultural nostalgia into a tool for critical reflection and genuine welcome. By reimagining hospitality as a dynamic, inclusive practice rooted in God's longing to dwell with humanity, communities can move beyond the limitations of the past and embody the radical love of Christ. At the same time, communities must acknowledge and permit others to hold onto their own reflective nostalgia for their original homes. True hospitality makes room for these diverse memories while offering space to create a new home together.

In doing so, the nostalgic longing for home finds its true fulfillment—not in recreating a bygone era, but in welcoming others to participate in God's home, as God dwells among us, and where all truly find a home.

SUGGESTIONS FOR FURTHER READING

Ahad-Legardy, Badia. *Afro-Nostalgia Feeling Good in Contemporary Black Culture.* New Black Studies. Urbana: University of Illinois Press, 2021.

Berry, David. *On Nostalgia.* Exploded Views. Toronto, ON: Coach, 2020.

Cassin, Barbara. *Nostalgia: When Are We Ever at Home?* Translated by Pascale-Anne Brault. New York: Fordham University Press, 2016.

McKay, Ian, and Robin Bates. *In the Province of History: The Making of the Public Past in Twentieth-Century Nova Scotia.* Montreal: McGill-Queen's University Press, 2010.

BIBLIOGRAPHY

Hofer, Johannes. "Medical Dissertation on Nostalgia, 1688." Translated by Carolyn Kiser Anspach. *Bulletin of the Institute of the History of Medicine* 2 (1934) 376–91. http://www.jstor.org/stable/44437799.

McKay, Ian, and Robin Bates. *In the Province of History: The Making of the Public Past in Twentieth-Century Nova Scotia.* Montreal: McGill-Queen's University Press, 2010.

Nova Scotia Commission on Building the Economy. *Now or Never: An Urgent Call to Action for Nova Scotians.* One Nova Scotia, Feb. 2014. https://www.onens.ca/sites/default/files/editor-uploads/now-or-never.pdf.

DISCUSSION QUESTIONS

1. What are some ways that nostalgia prevents your congregation from practicing authentic hospitality?

2. In what ways have you experienced God's "welcome home" in your life and church community?

3. How can your church better reflect authentic hospitality in its practices and spaces?

4. What steps can you take to listen to and amplify a wider diversity of voices in your community?

5

Hospitality and Your Health

Designed for Godly Character

GLEN BERRY

IT SEEMS ALMOST OBVIOUS to say that when we give to others we tend to feel good ourselves. Some get a "warm feeling"; others experience a sense of satisfaction or even joy. It is not as obvious why that is the case. Perhaps giving makes us feel good about ourselves. We like living up to an image we have of ourselves or being seen as someone with a benevolent character. Some might feel a sense of accomplishment because they demonstrate duty to their society or their faith. Still others take comfort in the old adage that "what goes around comes around," so it's worth making some kind of social investment. Phrases such as "pay it forward" or "put it out there in the universe" are common in recent years and suggest that many people expect fate to keep an account of such things. The *why* of giving may not always be obvious, but it does have a bearing on the giving process and the benefits to the giver. It may be even less obvious that there are many physical and mental health benefits for people who are givers.

BENEFITS OF HOSPITALITY

For years, research has shown that acts of kindness benefit both the recipient and the giver. The recipient gets support, gifts, and care. The giver, particularly if they are generous in their kindness, receives benefits to both their mental and physical health. Beyond the idea of a "warm feeling," this can include an improved mood. Usually this means something along the lines of better self-esteem or a stronger sense of well-being. It also includes improvement in feelings of depression, anxiety, and stress, even when these are at clinical levels. There are also physical benefits, such as reduced blood pressure and fewer or less intense aches and pains. This can also include better sleep and stronger immune functioning. As far as we know, these benefits don't depend on what is being given. It doesn't have to be something expensive. It doesn't even have to be anything material. It seems to be the kindness of the giving itself that matters. This phenomenon seems to be particularly pronounced when there is no expectation of a gift in return. It's as if the body (and the mind) don't really register an act as giving if the person is likely to receive something in return.

I am not suggesting that we should show kindness and hospitality to have better health, but these things seem connected. Human beings really seem to be designed for kindness. Our brains contain "mirror neurons" that activate when we see something happening to another person or they behave in a certain way. Among other things, this helps us empathize with others and more quickly imagine ourselves in their situation at an emotional level. Not everyone responds to every neural impulse of this kind, but the capacity is there in the overwhelming majority of us.

Scientists often argue that being "hardwired" this way is good for the species. It makes us more aware of and sensitive to the needs of others, as others are to us. Essentially, a community with the instinct to look after one another will do better than a community that does not.

This view is not without merit. There certainly has been clear research on societies benefiting from caring for each other.

Many would say that our health is the result of our genetics or the quality of our diet and exercise routines. True enough. But beyond these, about a dozen social and environmental factors play a strong role in the degree to which individuals or communities are healthy. Food security, housing security, transportation and access, and social inclusion are among them. I highlight these in particular because they are problems in the Atlantic provinces, but also because of their overlap with hospitality. Factors such as these contribute to how healthy we might be, how sick we might get, or even how long we might live. At some level, even our genes respond to the environment around us. An entire field of study—epigenetics—is dedicated to this connection. The degree to which we look after each other in these ways has an impact on our health and well-being.

Of course, the opposite is also true. When our neighbourhoods become sick, we all suffer. As we know from the recent pandemic, services and the economy do decline in sick neighbourhoods. The situation is the same in poor neighbourhoods, with limited access to services. There is often a higher rate of crime, mental health problems, and addictions. When we neglect our neighbours, and when our society does not provide needed services, our health and well-being decline, and we are more likely to die sooner. Our social world, then, is a significant determinant of our physical and mental health. More than we are likely aware, we live in an economy of reciprocal social interactions. A community with the instinct to look after one another will collectively do better than a community that does not.

Maybe we look after each other, or maybe we support the idea that our society does so because it ends up benefitting all of us in the long run. Smaller communities in Atlantic Canada have some experience of this, although more so in the past than today. People within our communities used to be more dependent upon each other. There was a type of local economy where everyone somehow contributed goods or services. It also made sense to look after others because you might need their help at some point. Reaping what you sow—perhaps that is simply the way of the world when at its best. It makes sense that we are designed to show hospitality to each other.

I would suggest, though, that the health benefits associated with kindness point to an even deeper connection than this. While there are clear benefits to a society that develops a system to look after one another, this still represents a set of reciprocal transactions where givers expect hospitality in return. Health benefits seem to be stronger when there is no expectation of reciprocity and when we are the ones giving.

THE LIMITS OF RECIPROCAL HOSPITALITY

There are limitations to offering kindness or hospitality with a reciprocal framework, where we expect it will ultimately be better for us if we help others. For example, there is a human tendency to most want to help people who are like us. We prefer to support our own. We can also be open to supporting people who do not look like us, provided that they act like us. We are less open to helping or even connecting with people who do things differently than us. It takes more effort for us to be helpful to *different* people. This may limit the kind of hospitality we offer others, despite biblical exhortations to "welcome the foreigner" (e.g., Lev 19:34). The hospitality we give too often depends on the feeling of sameness. However, we aren't all born with the same social status and privileges. If we feel that people with "less" are different than us, we may fail to offer them hospitality. This leads to those in need—who are different—remaining in need.

There is another limitation to communities that operate in an economy of reciprocity. Where churches were once often the center of helping those in need, governments have typically taken over this task. The concern here is that many of us think that is enough. Caring for the sick, looking after those experiencing poverty or homelessness, welcoming strangers—some might ask—"Isn't that what our government social programs are for?" Through taxes, we contribute to these programs to some degree, and they take care of these things for us to some degree.

In fact, our society benefits from showing hospitality to newcomers. For example, the Atlantic provinces have recently invited immigrants who have arguably had a positive impact on the economy. In Nova Scotia, the economy was given a fairly dismal forecast ten years ago. Despite some ongoing challenges, it has done better than predicted, and one major reason has been increased immigration. Debates continue about the future of immigration to Atlantic Canada, but at its best and worst, this openness to immigration is guided by selecting people who will contribute to our economy. We give to these people because they will help us.

In contrast, many churches have sponsored refugees from situations of war, famine, and hardship, with no concern for mutual benefit. They have made room, welcomed, and cared for those who happened to be born elsewhere. These churches understand that if we leave it to a government or an organization to care for those in need, we separate ourselves from the kindness of hospitality. We may hope or trust that things within our society go a certain way, but we won't be participating in it.

Taking this idea further, we exhibit hypocrisy when we express strong feelings about issues such as crime, the economy, abortion, or medical assistance in dying (MAID) and yet do nothing to support people facing those situations or to address the circumstances that contribute to those difficulties. How are we providing community opportunities and demonstrating care and acceptance—including openness to those "from away"? How are we supporting those needing housing, food, or other resources to care for their children? What about help with the suffering in life that contributes to some people's decision to choose death? Certainly, this would not change every situation, but our lack of involvement in these areas contributes to the pain associated with them. We separate ourselves from the personal responsibility of caring for others when we expect systems and governments to do it for us.

So the idea of "what goes around comes around" has limitations and doesn't go very far when we are selective about who we help or leave it to others to offer assistance. But the key here is that hospitality goes beyond supplying goods and services. It is a kind of social glue that provides cohesion and connection with others. It shows people that they are valued and ties us more tightly together. And remember, it is the individuals who provide this hospitality who benefit.

Also, keep in mind that health benefits seem to result only when we don't expect any reciprocity. Think about it like this: we likely don't necessarily get a "warm feeling" when we read about a new housing project or a food bank opening, even when we might be very much in favour of it. We don't get any health benefits from it either. Hospitality is more than just an economy of reciprocal transactions with each other. After all, even sinners do that:

> If you love those who love you, what credit is that to you? Even sinners love those who love them. And if you do good to those who are good to you, what credit is that to you? Even sinners do that. And if you lend to those from whom you expect repayment, what credit is that to you? Even sinners lend to sinners, expecting to be repaid in full. But love your enemies, do good to them, and lend to them without expecting to get anything back. Then your reward will be great, and you will be children of the Most High, because he is kind to the ungrateful and wicked. Be merciful, just as your Father is merciful. (Luke 6:32–36 NIV)

What does it say of us as individuals and churches when we expect a return on our hospitality from others, even if it is just for them to become more like us? Perhaps the opportunities given to us to help others are for the purpose of shaping our hearts as much as reshaping others. In giving to others, we open ourselves to God to grow us. If "what goes around comes around" is karma, then mercy and grace travel outside of karma.

HOSPITALITY AND CHARACTER

God calls us to do good for others and to offer hospitality when there is no obvious benefit to us. We are called to do this when we might not be thanked, when others won't start to become like us, and even when we can't guarantee the gift will be helpful or used responsibly in the long term. We see this in Luke 17:

> Now on his way to Jerusalem, Jesus traveled along the border between Samaria and Galilee. As he was going into a village, ten men who had leprosy met him. They stood at a distance and called out in a loud voice, "Jesus, Master, have pity on us!" When he saw them, he said, "Go, show yourselves to the priests." And as they went, they were cleansed. One of them, when he saw he was healed, came back, praising God in a loud voice. He threw himself at Jesus' feet and thanked him—and he was a Samaritan. Jesus asked, "Were not all ten cleansed? Where are the other nine? Has no one returned to give praise to God except this foreigner?" Then he said to him, "Rise and go; your faith has made you well." (vv. 11–19 NIV)

The ten lepers were healed, but only one came back to thank Jesus. We have no information that suggests the other nine changed their lives. Things likely went better for them after being healed, but there is no hint that any of them became godlier or even recognized God's favour on themselves, except for the one who returned to thank Jesus. I don't know how much foresight was in Jesus' mind when he encountered the lepers, but certainly God the Father would have known that most of them would not change. He knew that they would not become disciples or powerful witnesses or even be grateful. Yet he healed them anyway. God is compassionate, so Jesus showed compassion and called us to do the same. Ultimately, Jesus gave of himself without any guarantee that we would accept him or decide to change our lives.

Jesus asks us to go further than to help only when we have a guaranteed result. He also tells us to do good without our left hand knowing what the right hand is doing (Matt 6:3). He wants us to be mindful of our motives so they are grounded in the compassion and love of God. He wants to protect us from the distraction of how our image might look to others.

Jackie Pullinger is the founder of the St. Stephen's Society, a mission that began in Hong Kong and now has a broader reach. She has for decades spread the love of God through kind deeds to the hungry, victims of trafficking, those with substance use disorders, and those experiencing homelessness. In her work, she distinguishes between hospitality and aid and emphasizes that we often use the latter to replace the giving of ourselves, of our hearts. The difference here is that people may receive food or assistance, but lives don't change because of aid. They change from love. We share the heart of God through personal giving. So, how far do we take this, and who exactly are we supposed to do this for? Perhaps this question could be rephrased as: Who is my neighbour?

Consider the good Samaritan (Luke 10:25–37), who helped a man in need even though he was different than him. It is worth noting that he gave his own blanket and his own donkey (not the government's nor the church's). He took responsibility to show mercy because the opportunity was in front of him. Now imagine if those who had robbed the man had been somehow charged and brought to justice by authorities. It would have been wonderful if the society had responded in this way. Even still, the man who fell among the robbers would have encountered the love of God, mercy, and value from the Samaritan who gave of himself, not from a system, court, or government.

NEXT STEPS IN HOSPITALITY

There is no question that systems and societies that are just and provide for people are good things. However, we are all aware that government programs do not cover all the needs. In a lot of ways, we in Atlantic Canada lag behind much of the rest of the country in terms of social factors that lead to good health. Partly due to a lower population and partly due to less wealth, our services aren't as comprehensive as they might be in denser areas. There is room for the church to reclaim its role in helping the communities around us.

So, what might this mean for us as individuals or churches? It is worth taking stock of our attitudes and our hearts. How open are we to those who are in need or to those who are different than us?

Does it matter if they are from a different country, or which one? Does it matter if they are from a different race or different religion than us? Does it matter if they are experiencing poverty or homelessness? Does it matter if they have mental health problems or addictions? The question, "Who is your neighbour?" is quite different than, "Whom do you hang out with?" We have to push ourselves a little harder to accept people who are different than us.

Second, it is worth examining why we are doing this. We need to remember that hospitality means giving love rather than just goods or supplies. As Christians, we are called to show hospitality without looking for reciprocation or reward. We are called to do this by giving of ourselves. Even our biology seems to be geared towards this, with the health benefits that hospitality provides. This is what we were designed to do.

SUGGESTIONS FOR FURTHER READING

Oord, Thomas Jay. *Defining Love: A Philosophical, Scientific, and Theological Engagement.* Ada, MI: Brazos, 2010.

Pullinger, Jackie, and Andrew Quicke. *Chasing the Dragon: One Woman's Struggle Against the Darkness of Hong Kong's Drug Dens.* Rev. ed. Bloomington, MN: Chosen, 2007.

Sorokin, Pitirim A. *Ways & Powers of Love: Techniques of Moral Transformation.* West Conshohocken, PA: Templeton, 2002.

Squires, Veronica, and Breanna Lathrop. *How Neighborhoods Make Us Sick: Restoring Health and Wellness to Our Communities.* Lisle, IL: InterVarsity, 2019.

Wilkinson, Samuel T. *Purpose: What Evolution and Human Nature Imply About the Meaning of Our Existence.* New York: Pegasus, 2024.

DISCUSSION QUESTIONS

1. Who are the "neighbours" in need in your area?
2. What are some personal barriers to engaging with them?
3. What resources might you or your church community have to offer?
4. What do you think about "personal giving"?

6

Beyond Transactions

Hospitality as an Expression of Grace

CHRIS KILLACKY

BEFORE WE DELVE INTO the East Coast's take on hospitality, it's worth taking a quick snapshot of why hospitality has been in the news in recent years.

On the macro level, hospitality is probably best understood by its commercial application to the world and to us as individuals. The Conversation reported in 2022 that "bad managers, burnout and health fears" have caused record numbers of people to leave a career in hospitality.[1] Granted, the commercial application of paid hospitality is different than the biblical understanding of love given for free. Nevertheless, the large-scale abandonment of vocations in the hospitality industry perhaps enables us to start our own conversation about the rewards and obligations of hospitality in today's society.

The news media and blogosphere are full of commentary on the declining understanding and experience of hospitality in Western society, particularly North America, which, of course,

---

1. Moreo et al., "Bad Managers."

includes the East Coast of Canada. In its wider application, hospitality—or the breakdown of it—contributes to an inability to listen to another's opinion or to articulate one's own opinion in a moderate, respectful, and factual way.

Hospitality, then, has several layers and nuances. But at its base level, hospitality is an experience of welcome or goodwill between two or more people that involves receiving and responding to that experience. At this point another issue is whether a human can receive hospitality from a machine—but that is for another discussion. The idea of a relationship, no matter how temporary, that forms the basis of hospitality characterizes the reality of relationships on the East Coast. In addition to the nature of hospitality, this chapter examines the bonds, agreements, and expectations associated with hospitality; the responsibilities of the parties involved in offering and receiving hospitality; and what this all has to do with faith.

THE NATURE OF HOSPITALITY

Should you ask a passerby in the street what hospitality means to them, they would likely pause before answering. Most people do not think about deliberate acts of hospitality; rather, these acts often result from emotional responses of pity, sorrow, or anger at injustice—feelings rather than premeditated strategies. Indeed, deliberate hospitality strategies can often have a transactional rather than a relational quality, altering the nature of the expectations between the two parties.

Hospitality generally means to people things like offering a stranger a car ride, giving someone who is hungry food, welcoming new neighbours, and showing kindness and love to those who are less fortunate than ourselves. These responses, however, are usually one-time events that do not require much investment of time and resources, nor is there any expectation of a response. This type of hospitality tends to be one way, downward, and non-consequential. This generally has been a characteristic of East Coast hospitality. In our region, these superficial acts of hospitality fulfill a popular cultural image of East Coast people—kilt-wearing airport greeters and newcomer basket givers.

In the cases mentioned above, there are no substantial relationships between those offering the hospitality and those receiving it. It is really extending a tradition, rather than an act of personal welcome that builds a connection. Shared experiences—not transactions—create relationships, and a community is formed from many shared experiences by a group of people over time. At the far end of relationshipless engagements are the tourist experiences that offer the opportunity to experience the East Coast, wear the hoodie, and eat the food. These transactions have little substance and can foster only two things: first, the anticipation of joining red-haired Celtic fiddlers around warm log fires with bowls of scallops and lobster broth washed down by the craftiest of East Coast beers. Second, the disappointment and emptiness that these images are a veneer that is not really lived—these are for the tourists, and experiencing them requires newly exchanged Canadian dollars. In this sense, the East Coast is no different than any other "destination" that seeks to exploit the memories of past communities among those who wish to glimpse the fantasy of them for a short season—and to say or feel that they were "an East Coaster." Here, the only expectation is a return on investment on the one side and an emotional photo opportunity on the other.

What, then, and where are the real acts and experiences of hospitality? How can hospitality spread and become a reality with a substantial and enduring impact that grows a community? Hospitality is the bedrock of community.

The Christian tradition talks about hospitality and deep-seated respect for one another. This emerges from the idea that all humans are made in the image of God, the imago Dei. This understanding both levels us all to a common plane and causes us to grapple with the reality that we bear a responsibility of action and reaction to each other.

The East Coast is steeped in Christian heritage and tradition. One needs only to survey the landscape to see this, the fabric of Christendom—its spires, graveyards, and quaint white churches speak to a maritime youth full of Sunday Schools, Christian camps, and congregations busily making their way to worship God. The DNA of a Christian lifestyle is encoded on the East Coast. The heart of this DNA is the gospel and its message of love and responsibility. This is the essence of hospitality and the standard by which acts are measured and even defined as being hospitable. Whether this Christian topography has lived up to the high calling expected of the Christian calling is another topic, one that highlights the reality of the apostle Paul's knowing what he should do and yet also knowing that he does not live up to that standard.

THE BONDS, AGREEMENTS, AND EXPECTATIONS OF HOSPITALITY

Christianity is a religion full of grace. It involves a free giving of love, including an obligation to do good to one's neighbour. Christians once commonly practiced feeding the poor, welcoming strangers, and even sharing song and food in the heart of the home through events like the kitchen party. Yet it's easy to say that grace in some way contradicts the idea of responsibility, which is untrue. Gifts made of grace also bear great responsibility. They are not transactional; the giver of hospitality should not necessarily expect a personal reward, nor is the recipient of grace forced to respond with a token of appreciation. The mere act is spiritually uplifting and is often encouraged to be done in secret, the implication being that God will reward the giver openly. Nevertheless, the benefits of grace are caught up in the nature of the relationship that is forged through the act of giving. The recipient, having thankfully received such a gift, is reminded of the nature of this grace, encouraged, and warmed to respond likewise. In doing so, gradually the whole community experiences love and care. Relationships are then formed and bonds are created. This forms a covenant, spoken or unspoken, between those who during their lives are either givers or recipients of grace—hopefully both.

The expression of Christian love to the stranger is an expression of hospitality. The example of airport "greeters" and "givers" has no true relationship substance and fails to reflect the Christian understanding of community, love, and covenant based upon a sense of goodness that flows from the inner soul. True hospitality offers hope both within and beyond traditional Christian communities that helps form wholesome groups, sanctifies the land, and makes up a society underpinned by the same premise of grace and love. True hospitality does not operate on a reward-based system, but on a framework pinned by Christian values, where work and reward are not connected by a direct line. True hospitality is a way to generate community based upon something that emanates from a wholly good God. For grace is not the work—not by the recipient, anyway. Rather, grace should be seen as a foundation of hospitality that brings value to both the giver and receiver.

THE RESPONSIBILITIES OF HOSPITALITY

Although we have separated work and reward and introduced grace as a basis on which the East Coast emerged under Christian influence, let us also consider the responsibilities that accompany grace and, by association, apply them to hospitality. The benefits of reciprocal expressions of grace are that both parties engage in unselfish acts of common understanding and expectation. Those who receive but choose not to contribute in return—rather those who can't—eventually cannot benefit spiritually from the society and community to which they belong. The Bible speaks of the blessings that come from giving and not holding back. Without reciprocity, the line and theme of grace are broken. This does not mean that grace should not continue to be offered to all, but that it is impossible for those who do not embrace the gift and pass it on to benefit from it. In a real sense, they become outsiders. They have received only an outward gift rather than a gift that benefits both the body and soul.

Beyond the superficial acts of hospitality that characterize the East Coast in media and tourist centers, the region benefits from the residue of a former Christian heritage, one based upon this understanding of grace. While nostalgia can at times be "rose tinted," there has been in recent years a revival of the "Nova Scotia Strong" character, one that overcomes challenges and pushes forward in the face of a Nor'easter. The idea of coming together to face adversity represents an attempt to support the weakest in society and is an outward expression of community, one defined by shared griefs and bonds. The East Coast is good at this and has over recent years faced various tragedies with courage. But how real is the substance of hospitality on the East Coast today? How friendly are neighbours to newcomers? How do the benefits of hospitality appear in today's society? Has the East Coast become only an echo of those Christian values of graceful hospitality— just another part of secular North America? Further, in what ways do those who receive this gracious hospitality embrace and pass it on in both body and soul?

The answers to these provocative questions are not to be found in the smugglers' inns and ceilidhs of Nova Scotia's tourist trade. Nor are the answers likely to trip off the tongue of a person walking down a maritime main street. The question is possibly best answered by looking at how that Christian echo of grace has responded to the arrival of thousands of newcomers, mostly from other parts of Canada but also from international immigration, since the recent pandemic. For it was during the pandemic that the world and certainly Canada discovered the Maritimes, that hidden place of lobsters and brightly coloured houses built mostly using no builder's square nor level.

The assertion that society is broken is no longer bold but commonplace, including in relation to the East Coast. This statement has many meanings to many people, but to me, it means that the fabric of grace and Christian heritage within the East Coast has been diminished to such an extent that relationships no longer have shared experiences that bond them. There is across the Western world a rising concern about ethnicity, immigration, and the perceived inability of newcomers to fit in. This has recently been compounded in Canada by a housing shortage that the federal government is associating with immigration and student visas to the extent that it has reduced both considerably.

How, then, is hospitality, something based upon the idea of grace, able to thrive in a less hospitable world?

HOSPITALITY AND CHRISTIAN FAITH

The ability of a society to respond effectively to brokenness has always consisted of two parts: a spiritual part and a physical part—an integral approach. This approach also exhibits grace, and it is that aspect of grace that I argue contributes to hospitality on the East Coast. But now that we see Christianity in decline, those spired reminders of the community of grace now vacant, it is difficult to see that society can be restored. The basic understanding of our responsibility both to give and to respond has been eroded, even secularized into a commodity-driven transactional parody of a once mostly hospitable and gracious response found across communities on the East Coast. With secularism and post-Christian societal development comes an understanding of the world as a material realm, one without the immaterial, a body without a soul. In such a secular society the Christian perspective is challenged and there is no understanding of the inward blessings that accompany acts of grace-filled hospitality. Everything simply becomes an empty transaction of material benefit alone, or at best of some emotional good that derives from the satiation of the conscience—an attempt to remedy the guilt of having something that others do not. If the benefits of hospitality are outward, they do not resonate with the inward, immaterial song of the soul: joy, peace, goodness, and love, qualities that are based upon faith ignited by the Holy Spirit. Whether one agrees or disagrees that the Spirit of God can work only in the believer, the responsibility to help meet the needs of society through hospitality seems to have been lost somehow. The brokenness that pervades society is not healed by material hospitality, nor do those who receive it gain deep satisfaction. Moreover, not having received in their soul the real spiritual benefit of hospitality, the recipients are unable to pass it on in its purest sense. Hospitality of this sort is but a shell and veneer of the fullness that hospitality should be. It is a de-Christianized parody of the real thing. The historic Christian confessions of the Reformation understand this, as they address the "good works" of those from whom the Spirit of God is absent. They conclude that while there are common goods or graces—civil kindnesses—good works outside of Christ differ from those done through faith. This idea challenges us to consider the root of our own hospitality.

Fr. Francis Xavier Lasance includes writings from Fr. William Faber in his early twentieth-century book *My Prayer Book.* He writes about the kindness that is not external and hollow, but that is principally an internal act that also manifests itself externally. It is something that comes from the soul. Other forms of apparent kindness are empty and a false facade.[2] In the light of these words, it is a worthy exercise to take honest stock of the East Coast. At a fundamental level, I ask, is it even possible for a society that has become increasingly godless and soulless to offer anything other than the empty kindness that Fr. Lasance speaks of? Is the hospitality that a spiritually dead society offers nothing more than the polished, perfect smile of a wealthy North American—trained to shine at the right moments, shaped through unnatural braces, maintained with meticulous flossing, and whitened with paste—giving an appearance that exudes happiness? (For that is what a smile suggests, we are trained to believe.) There is a tendency to understand responsibility as a collective endeavour, as measuring all the ingredients in a single kitchen cup, or the whole of society by one trait. East Coast society may indeed have collectively lost its savour. Yet, looking or tasting more deeply with the palette of a spiritual gourmet, perhaps those few grains of salt, the remaining faithful Christians dotted here and there, can prevent the whole chowder from being inedible. Perhaps Fr. Lasance's empty society is not entirely soulless, but the menu consists of fish cakes rather than lobster. The answer lies somewhere in the blur between inward intention and outward expression.

If we no longer measure the substance of hospitality in outward acts but rather as inward acts that also erupt outwardly, how much better will the reward within the soul be? Defined in these

2. Lasance, *My Prayer-Book,* 65.

terms, hospitality now has meaning. This causes us to think about why we are doing the act of kindness and not simply the act itself. We realize that in addition to soul kindness, there is also empty kindness, a hollow hospitality that neither has inward benefits nor can be a balm to the brokenness of a society void of its Christian soul. Who and what, then, are these empty forms of kindness? They emanate from places that seek to satisfy only material needs—government social services and places of worship that do not speak a true gospel but focus on good works that are not sourced in the fountain of eternal life, Jesus Christ. These types of kindness cannot provide what truly satisfies eternally, but only that which feeds the body for a short time. For some, it is a well-meaning desire to alleviate the needs of those less fortunate, for some it gains political credit, and for some it satisfies the conscience and balances the book of things that ought to have been done. Yet, for all, we must be wary that the hospitality we share is not empty and that our soul giving is not dead, for when the government is secular, and when the religion worships a god who does not live, there is all the more reason to shine Christ's light brightly.

The rewards and obligations from entering into hospitality are many, yet they are received and truly given in their fullest quality only by those who have a living faith. Of course, we cannot judge nor discern those in whom faith lives, nor are we to divide the wheat from the tares. The Lord knows his people, the East Coast agate and jewels of Christ, the people of God, who have been given good works to do by a living God who has prepared these works ahead of them, and we are told that these good works are done in obedience to God (Eph 2:10). There is only one living and true faith, and this is Christianity. While many people perform good and helpful actions, those people, systems, and religions that do works founded not in the living soul but in human conscience are of no eternal spiritual benefit. They may, in the economy of God's providence, be useful civil blessings that work to a greater goal unseen to us, for their fruit lies beyond the hills obscuring our sight. Yet, works that were not prepared by God are similitudes of good works or, as Fr. Lasance says, empty forms of kindness. It is not a huge leap to deduce that in a society that is no longer Christian, people cannot, to the same degree, do the works of eternal value that God has prepared for them—that is to say, immaterial and substantial works of kindness—of which hospitality is one. In saying this, I also acknowledge that Christians at times have failed in their responsibility to those around them, to the peoples who were often less fortunate than the majority, to Black populations, and to Indigenous peoples. The light of hospitality has at times been dimmed with selfishness and unawareness.

How, then, can we be hospitable and kind in a way that has value and substance? We must bring out this character from within; it cannot be only on the surface. It must also emanate from true faith in order to be the fullness of what it should be. Without this, any form of hospitality is but a shadow of the real thing.

For those who receive only the empty veneer of East Coast hospitality, there is benefit only in a material sense; it will not sustain nor last, nor bring deep satisfaction. Neither can the giver gain inwardly from such empty hospitality. No matter how much flossed the smile, it cannot match that of the un-dentistried, crooked but warm, loving beam of the soul-filled face of grace. For those who have received kindness from such a soul, works that were prepared by God beforehand, there is also a responsibility to respond in faith first and then through works. The response to these honest good works is one of thankfulness to a gracious God, turning to and serving him. There is no other reasonable response.

The East Coast still has dotted throughout its land a residue of faith, and there are still good works prepared for God's people to do. The joy of giving and receiving hospitality can be rich and full again if experienced through living faith in Jesus Christ. If we fix our faith, the rest will follow. But without faith and the loving gifting of hospitality in Christ, all that can be expected is a muted form of kindness, uninhabited by God's Spirit, and desolate of depth. Yet this doesn't have to be the last chapter. God can still feed us with the few fish that are brought to the hillside, still fill our twelve baskets with the finest lobster, and still work the enduring miracle of salvation with heartfelt hospitality. How can we rise to that challenge?

SUGGESTIONS FOR FURTHER READING

Lacey, Carolyn. *Extraordinary Hospitality (For Ordinary People): Seven Ways to Welcome Like Jesus.* UK: Good Book, 2021.

VanDoodewaard, Rebecca. *How Should I Exercise Hospitality? Cultivating Biblical Godliness.* Grand Rapids: Reformation Heritage, 2017.

Wilkins, Steve. *Face to Face: Meditations on Friendship and Hospitality.* Moscow, ID: Canon, 2010.

BIBLIOGRAPHY

Lasance, F. X. *My Prayer-Book: Happiness in Goodness; Reflections, Counsels, Prayers, and Devotions.* New York: Benziger Bros., 1908. https://archive. org/details/myprayerbookhappoooolasa.

Moreo, Andrew, et al. "Bad Managers, Burnout and Health Fears: Why Record Numbers of Hospitality Workers Are Quitting the Industry for Good." Conversation, Jan. 31, 2022; updated Feb. 2, 2022. https://theconversation. com/bad-managers-burnout-and-health-fears-why-record-numbers-of-hospitality-workers-are-quitting-the-industry-for-good-174588.

DISCUSSION QUESTIONS

1. How can your church community help offer sanctuary to newcomers who are having government hospitality withdrawn from them through cancellation of visas?

2. Do you think that the secularization of society has caused people to lose sight of the source of hospitality—God's love and grace?

3. What do you think of the idea of responsibilities accompanying Christian hospitality? How might this impact your own hospitality?

7

For Our Future Churches

Education as Hospitality

JODI L. PORTER

I AM NOT A native of Wolfville, Nova Scotia, nor even of Atlantic Canada, yet in some ways, my newly adopted home is already a familiar place for me. I'm from corn fields near a stellar liberal arts college. I'm from a small, rural church with a heart for Jesus. I'm from lands still conflicted over their histories with colonization, slavery, and other modern injustices. And in my journeys thus far, I've engaged with several different ethnic and ecclesial cultures, many of which I also find here in the Annapolis Valley.

When my family was discerning whether to move to the valley for new roles at Acadia Divinity College, we noticed that Wolfville happens to be a wonderful combination of many of our favourite things. Oddly, it even happens to have the same three-digit phone prefix as my Midwestern American hometown, making me feel at home right away! And the community offers added bonuses as well. We didn't have the ocean view and tides, or the mountain ridges, near the corn fields where I played as a toddler and worked as a teen.

Throughout my journey, I've been a student of the church. Thanks to the Christian faith of my parents, I've attended church since before I knew how to speak or walk, growing up in a small congregation in north-central Missouri. When I attended that nearby liberal arts college, I opted to major in religious studies to focus the bulk of my time on (what I thought would be) learning why I believe what I believe. Actually, that experience led to an entirely different set of questions that have resulted in a lifelong pursuit of compelling Christian faith and institutions that cultivate such faith. My passion became nurturing fruitful conversations between the church and the academy.

It has long seemed to me that my faith, our faith, can be better (more faithful) with support from scholars' work in biblical, historical, and theological studies, as well as practical ministry. And at the same time, the academy's work is better when it is connected to the faithful efforts of the individuals and communities that comprise the church. Neither the church nor the academy makes sense, I would say, without the other as a conversation partner.

So, as my journey has continued, I've been not only a student of the church but also of education, capping off that passion with a doctoral degree. I centered my EdD program on leadership and organizational learning in the church and the academy. And through all my academic and professional experiences, which also include service in leadership education at Duke Divinity School and the Forum for Theological Exploration, I've learned (even if it sounds a bit cliché) that education is less about *knowing* the right things and more about *doing* the right things.

In a word, it's about hospitality.

THE FUTURING LAB

My colleague Joel Murphy and I lead the ADC Futuring Lab, where we hope to help shape possible, probable, and preferred futures for the church and for theological education. As we aim to inspire the imaginations of our constituencies, we first offer the disclaimer that we don't have a crystal ball. Instead, we are curating resources that can help theological schools and churches reflect on their contexts in ways that lead church and academy, and the relationship between the two, forward well. Essentially, we must listen to each other, within our contexts and beyond into the communities we serve, to take faithful next steps.

The Futuring Lab could suggest standardized responses to new challenges as they emerge. But why should our imaginations at ADC have all the say? It seems to me that the task of the lab is to offer resources that invite all voices within any given community to share thoughts and experiences, discerning their best choices together. And the best choice for one church or seminary may not be the best for another, because each community has its own challenges and opportunities to navigate.

Again, our educational work is a task of, in one word, hospitality.

My invitation in this chapter is to reflect on ways that not only our lab but also theological schools or churches generally can set the tables for this essential task for the future church. Whether we hail from Atlantic Canada, the Midwestern United States, or somewhere else entirely, the Spirit is waiting, speaking to each of us in our communities. If we don't take time to share with each other, really to listen to each other and discern carefully together, how can we hear God's voice for us? How can we hear God's hopes for our futures? How can we co-create those futures with God and our neighbours?

Before we reflect further on these questions, I'll share a short vignette to get us in the spirit of extending hospitality as we educate for the future.

LOOK, MOM! I SEE JESUS!

When we lived in Waco, Texas, our family lived in a neighbourhood comprised of people from several racial/ethnic backgrounds. In no small part, it was a neighbourhood of colour. We attended a Black Baptist congregation where the preacher shared robust sermons that often included praiseful shouting of the name of JESUS!

One weekday, I pushed my then-two-year-old daughter's stroller into the local post office, where the USPS advertisements looked like our friends in the community with Black and Brown faces. Loudly, my daughter shouted, "Look, Mom! I see Jesus!"

As I rushed to quiet her, I realized several things almost simultaneously. First, she thought our pastor, who called the name of Jesus so often, was named Jesus(!), and she thought she saw our pastor's face on the sign (two errors that, at first, I thought required embarrassed, immediate shushing). But then I smiled as I realized that even though she was making literally incorrect observations, she was exactly right—metaphorically. I, too, saw the face of Jesus in those faces on the sign. And in the people at the post office. And in all my neighbours. But not until my daughter took a moment amid our busy day to remind me.

And why quiet a child who's excited to see Jesus? Maybe her energy will be infectious! (My now-teenage daughter especially enjoys it when I tell this story these days.)

The mission of ADC's parent denomination, the Canadian Baptists of Atlantic Canada (CBAC), is to serve Jesus in our neighbourhoods today and tomorrow. Our hope at ADC is to prepare Christian leaders to serve the mission of God with transformative impact in the church and world. Both missions require us and all our constituents to listen well to each other. We must extend hospitality through the tables we set at ADC and in our churches. We must offer generous spaces for sharing, interpreting, and responding together to concerns and possibilities in our contexts. After all, you never know where one of us—or all of us—might spot Jesus!

What might it look like, then, to practice education as hospitality? We will take the rest of this chapter to explore that idea more specifically.

THE GOOD SHEPHERD AND WORLD COMMUNION

I have a special love for the Godly Play curriculum, designed by Jerome Berryman. The curriculum is based on the Montessori educational philosophy of self-driven exploration, inviting children (and adults!) to imagine themselves in biblical stories and ask open-ended, wondering questions about them. We ask: "I wonder . . . did God come close to you, or did you come close to God, in this story? I wonder . . . where is this story, really? What is the story really about, right now?" Godly Play story leaders share the stories, typically by utilizing various 3-D props on the floor, with listeners sitting with them in a circle. And every lesson ends with these wondering questions.

My favourite Godly Play story is that of the Good Shepherd and world communion. It is a liturgical story connecting Psalm 23 with the communion narratives of the New Testament, inviting participants to enter into those stories in ways that glean fresh insights. It starts with a Shepherd who looks after all his sheep in the sheepfold, with sheep who know his voice when he calls them by name. It shifts to a priest or pastor who offers communion at the table, representing the Good Shepherd to all his people in the world. The story is an invitation of hospitality to all people: to listen for God's voice, to come to God's table, and to invite others to come as well.[1]

Sometimes, children and adults have poignant ideas to share after hearing the story. Sometimes, the insights aren't what I would have expected. Most recently, when I shared the story at a small valley church, one participant (maybe three years old) shared his thoughts. When I asked, "Having experienced the story together, would anyone like to share something?," he replied, "Yes. I like to share my toys." In moments when I receive responses like that one, I resist my first reaction: a temptation to "correct" the child, saying, "That's not what the story is about." Because what if it is?

So, instead, I pause. I let my heart smile and my head reflect. I wouldn't have thought of that response. But what if that response is the child's best one in the moment? And what if the community needs that voice as they decide their best responses to the story right now? That's exactly why we must extend hospitality—not only to our young but to everyone—as we read Scripture. We are better in discerning together than on our own.

1. Berryman et al., *Godly Play*, 113–22.

As it turns out, the approach to Scripture espoused by Godly Play can be easily adapted to educate with hospitality in churches and seminary classrooms. In fact, it is one example of emerging models of education that center on hospitality.

CYCLES OF HOSPITALITY:
ACTIVE, COLLABORATIVE, INNOVATIVE

In recent decades, the leading edges of scholarship have been shifting from the passive "banking" model of education, involving "deposits" of information moving from teachers to students, to a more active model of education. That active model entails empowering students to articulate their circumstances and respond to them thoughtfully. Paulo Freire, an educator and philosopher from Brazil, called this approach that of cultivating critical consciousness (*conscientização*). Harvard educator Marshall Ganz developed an embodied version of this approach that emphasizes stories of self, us, and now.

This kind of approach does not rely on "sages on the stage" to dictate content or responses to questions. Instead, it is collaborative; it invites the "wisdom in the room" to emerge from all who are present. Rather than understanding knowledge as objective, it presumes all knowledge is situated within individual and communal experiences. It does not assume that a single instructor (or pastor!) knows all the answers but that communities can discover answers and effect innovative changes together.

On the one hand, such an approach to education can seem scary. I really would like someone just to tell me, already, what to believe and why. But on the other hand, such an approach to education is not only hospitable—it's freeing. It's even particularly Baptist. We espouse the priesthood of all believers, along with soul competency. We believe that the Spirit can speak through each of us so long as we listen well to Scripture and our lives, discerning in partnership with faithful community amid what we hear.

Explaining this active educational approach demystifies how we might explore the future(s) of theological education and the church with hospitality. As I've hinted already, we at the Futuring Lab are not going to read tea leaves for you (and I'm sure that's a relief). Instead, we hope to empower Christian leaders with at least two significant tools: our best research on emerging trends that might impact our institutions' future(s) and our best resources to help leaders identify and reflect on trends most pertinent in their contexts.

One resource commonly used in the organizational sciences is the PDSA (plan-do-study-act) improvement cycle, which helps analyze a current context and shape the next best steps. The cycle moves through steps of reflection and action, illuminating next improvements over small arcs of time. It emerged from the work of W. Edwards Deming and Toyota Motor Corporation to make better vehicles and new processes for production.[2]

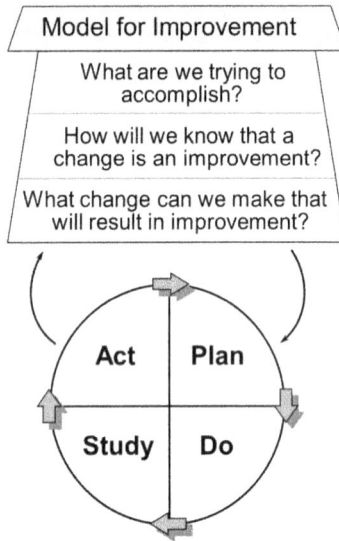

Model for Improvement[3]

---

2. See Rother, *Toyota Kata.*

3. Langley et al., *Improvement Guide*, 9.

The improvement cycle is the core idea these days for effective approaches to improvement in industries, including not only business but also education, health care, the military, and not-for-profit work. It was the core of my graduate doctoral experience. And it also can serve as the core of a hospitable approach to education or ministry as long as a community engages in the cycle together, listening and responding to all the "wisdom in the room."

Since I'm trained as an organizational theorist and practitioner, educator, and practical theologian, I notice versions of the cycle everywhere. The Maguerez Arch is an example of its application in education: the arch offers steps for students to observe reality, reflect on how to improve particular situations, and apply theories and hypotheses for positive change. The image on the following page illustrates its use for a course in nursing education focused on addictions. The arch illustrates how any leader might embody hospitality in the classroom or congregation by deemphasizing content on a topic and instead inviting self-guided, action-oriented research connected to community needs.

Arch of Maguerez

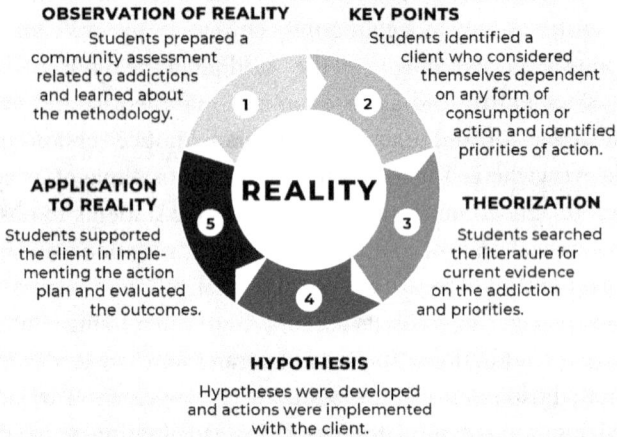

OBSERVATION OF REALITY
Students prepared a community assessment related to addictions and learned about the methodology.

KEY POINTS
Students identified a client who considered themselves dependent on any form of consumption or action and identified priorities of action.

APPLICATION TO REALITY
Students supported the client in implementing the action plan and evaluated the outcomes.

REALITY

THEORIZATION
Students searched the literature for current evidence on the addiction and priorities.

HYPOTHESIS
Hypotheses were developed and actions were implemented with the client.

Arch of Maguerez[4]

The pastoral cycle is an example of applying the improvement cycle in ministry. It contains simple steps for Christian leaders hoping to shape faithful actions via reflection on Christian Scripture, traditions, and unique contexts. This praxis model image on the following page depicts the core steps in the pastoral cycle. Leaders (1) try faithful actions ("committed action"); (2) reflect on them considering context, Scripture, and tradition ("reflection"); and (3/1) imagine next most faithful actions in a continuously repeating loop of reflective, committed action ("committed and intelligent action," or praxis).

4. Reisdorfer et al., "Heutagogy," 596.

The Praxis Model

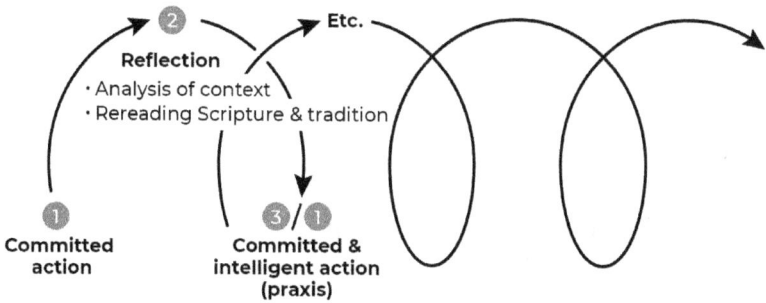

The Praxis Model[5]

I'd suggest the pastoral cycle is a resource that pastors and laity can adapt for several hospitable purposes. First, it should serve as the core model for our formation and discipleship efforts. It offers an easy way to illustrate the practice of theological reflection. It can shape individuals who are theologically literate not because they know the "right" answers but because they know how to utilize Scripture and Christian tradition well in their vocations. Second, it can function as an "improvement cycle" for church and academy, serving as a practical model for theologically reflective communities hoping to analyze their contexts and change as needed. And third, it can operate as an educational approach in seminary classrooms and ministry contexts, helping individuals and communities connect current trends and challenges with Christian resources for faithful future steps.

Whether we are growing as disciples, navigating trends in communities, or engaging in further education to help do God's work in the world, the pastoral cycle affords the hospitality to try our best, reflect with Christian imagination, and try again.

A model like the PDSA improvement cycle, and related educational and pastoral cycles, can help us here in Atlantic Canada and beyond seek Jesus in church and academy. These models help

5. Bevans, *Models of Contextual Theology*, 76.

us not clamour for the definite but rather lean into the not-fully-knowable Infinite together. And we can harness them for our work to shape the future church hospitably.

HOSPITABLE EDUCATION FOR FUTURE CHURCHES

Allow me to share one possible future scenario for the church. Our lab's facilitator for trend research and analysis, Joel Murphy, has posed this possible future by reflecting on trends such as increased online content, increased individualism, the influencer as an "expert," digital literacy, pluralism, and the changing role(s) of pastors.

With support from ChatGPT 4.0, Murphy has imagined the following:

> By the year 2035, Harmony Hills Church (an imaginary congregation) has experienced a profound spiritual metamorphosis under the guidance of Pastor Sheila, who has blended the roles of spiritual shepherd, digital discernment expert, and collaborative leader. Departing from traditional sermons, she has transformed the church into a relational and exploratory space. She curates opportunities for individuals to engage with biblical texts, modern philosophies, and emerging social media content, all via small groups (both in-person and virtual). Pastor Sheila prioritizes the responsibility of helping congregants to navigate the trustworthy and questionable content in the digital realm, focusing her time and energy on encouraging spiritual discernment and critical thinking among congregants. She also shares leadership responsibilities, empowering congregants to actively contribute to the church's vibrant discourse by encouraging vulnerability and discussion. The church has become a dynamic space for collaboration, where lively discussions, pastoral counselling, and shared leadership foster a community equipped to discern the complexities of the modern world with wisdom and purpose.

This possible future is one example of birthing the future church by approaching education as hospitality. In this scenario, the pastor is not functioning as the "sage on the stage" but rather the "shepherd on the side." Pastor Sheila is what we might call a "content curator" and a "community builder." She presumes her role is less about delivering content (by not emphasizing sermons) and more about shaping practices for collaborative leadership and discernment amid the digital content already out there. Is this future one you might like to imagine for your own congregation? Is this open-ended hospitality also possible in seminary classrooms (by not emphasizing lectures)?

If you are wondering how you might identify trends and discover educational ideas like these that can shape the future of your congregation or classroom, I'll share a few thoughts in this final section to get you started. Stay tuned to the lab website as we continue to curate more resources for Christian leaders.[6]

First, this is my adapted, expanded version of Godly Play: I like to leverage interactive resources that can help all of us raise our consciousness of God's work in our midst. If I am asked to lead a course, offer a workshop, or even lead a worship service, I am more likely to facilitate conversation than lecture or preach. (I sometimes do the other activities, but I prefer to couple them with more hospitable practices.) If I can offer tools that guide a community through a version of the improvement cycle for their own faithful work in the world, then I do.

Second, one of my favourite inspirations for hospitable education is a model created by my former workplace, the Forum for Theological Exploration. The model is called CARE, an acronym representing its key phases: creating hospitable space, asking self-awakening questions, reflecting theologically together, and enacting the next most faithful step.[7]

Finally, as a facilitator of hospitable education, I'd be remiss not to mention my favourite repositories of facilitation techniques. The websites IDEO U and The Art of Hosting both offer resources

6. www.acadiadiv.ca/sandbox.

7. For more on this approach, see Lewis et al., *Another Way*.

in collaborative, human-centered design.[8] The activities included in these resources focus on participant involvement, inviting participants to name topics, brainstorm resources, and create responses. In her recent book, *Innovating for Love: Joining God's Expedition Through Christian Social Innovation*, Kenda Creasy Dean (ADC Simpson Lecturer for 2025) reflects on what can be a scary topic—innovation—and describes it for Christian contexts as something familiar. She suggests that Christian innovation centers the call to love Christ every day, step by step. Because embodying this call most faithfully in the future (or even present) might require revising or replacing some of our traditional practices, she includes an appendix of exercises to guide organizations—playfully—through tough conversations for change.[9]

CONCLUSION

To be transparent, I'm not sure our future churches will be all that different than our past and present churches. But let me clarify what I mean by that. As Creasy Dean suggests, the Christian mission always has been the same: to embody Jesus' love in who we are and what we do. However, doing so in our most faithful ways *must* change from century to century, decade to decade, even year to year and day to day. Our structures and practices cannot stay the same as the world changes. Our core focus can stay the same, but we must respond to the challenges and opportunities of each new day.

For example, how can we understand and share God's story compellingly in increasingly post-Christian and politically polarized cultures? How can we respond to historic and persistent complicities with injustice among local Indigenous communities? What can intercultural ministry look like as more immigrants join our neighbourhoods and churches in Atlantic Canada? What can

8. www.ideou.com; www.artofhosting.com.

9. Creasy Dean, *Innovating for Love*.

education and ministry look like as revolutionary technologies like generative artificial intelligence emerge?

Though it is not the church's vocation to be "trendy," God has commissioned us (in Acts 1:8) to share the good news to the ends of the earth, through the Spirit. And we must figure out how to do so in *each* new season, in our own contexts. Maybe our structures for churches, or ministries, or Sunday morning activities are no longer fit for their intended purposes. Maybe our structures for seminaries, or programs, or teaching are no longer fit for their intended purposes. How do we know what pieces to keep, abandon, adapt, or create?

I contend, again, that there will not be one way forward for church and academy but multiple ways forward. And we will discover and shape those ways most fruitfully if we work together through hospitable educational practices. We can leverage versions of the improvement cycle and resources centering play, facilitation, and innovation to help us have the conversations that can guide us forward . . . to look for Jesus in unexpected places like the post office . . . to welcome the most creative responses to any biblical story . . . to set tables for active, collaborative conversations about innovative next steps in our neighbourhoods.

For our future, education must function as hospitality in all the churches and schools we call home.

SUGGESTIONS FOR FURTHER READING

Ballard, Paul, and John Pritchard. *Practical Theology in Action: Christian Thinking in the Service of Church and Society.* 2nd ed. London: SPCK, 2006.

Benac, Dustin D. *Adaptive Church: Collaboration and Community in a Changing World.* Waco: Baylor University Press, 2022.

Creasy Dean, Kenda. *Innovating for Love: Joining God's Expedition Through Christian Social Innovation.* Greatest Expedition. Knoxville: Market Square, 2021.

Lewis, Stephen, et al. *Another Way: Living & Leading Change on Purpose.* Danvers, MA: Chalice, 2020.

BIBLIOGRAPHY

Berryman, Jerome, et al. *The Complete Guide to Godly Play: Volume 4*. Rev. and expanded ed. New York: Church Publishing, 2018.

Bevans, Stephen B. *Models of Contextual Theology*. Rev. ed. Faith and Cultures. Maryknoll, NY: Orbis, 2002.

Creasy Dean, Kenda. *Innovating for Love: Joining God's Expedition Through Christian Social Innovation*. Greatest Expedition. Knoxville: Market Square, 2021.

Langley, Gerald J., et al. *The Improvement Guide: A Practical Approach to Enhancing Organizational Performance*. 2nd ed. San Francisco: Wiley, 2009.

Lewis, Stephen, et al. *Another Way: Living & Leading Change on Purpose*. Danvers, MA: Chalice, 2020.

Reisdorfer, Emilene, et al. "Heutagogy: A Pedagogical Framework for Cultivating Critical Consciousness in Nursing Students." *International Journal of Caring Sciences* 17 (2024) 593–602. https://www.international journalofcaringsciences.org/docs/59.reisdorfer.pdf.

Rother, Mike. *Toyota Kata: Managing People for Improvement, Adaptiveness, and Superior Results*. New York: McGraw Hill, 2009.

DISCUSSION QUESTIONS

1. What comes to mind for you and others at your church when you hear the word "educate"? What might it look like for your church to pursue education with even more hospitality than you do currently?

2. How might you utilize the pastoral cycle in your work to . . .

   a. cultivate theologically literate and reflective Christian leaders?

   b. improve your current church practices and ministries?

   c. help your organization respond to a particular cultural trend?

3. How might you use new approaches to play, facilitation, or innovation to help your church shape faithful futures?

8

From Hostility to Hospitality

Intentionally Cultivating a Multiethnic Congregation in a Historically Monoethnic Church

CARLEY LEE

THOUGH THE BELL RANG to signal the start of the day, a group of teens sat stubbornly on the lawn, watching their classmates stream into the school, waiting for the media to arrive.

They were junior high students—thirteen, fourteen, and fifteen years old, filled with teenage angst and righteous indignation in the way only young people can be. But though their youth may well have contributed to their volatility, their anger and frustration were no less justified.

One of these students was thirteen-year-old Lennett Anderson, who was drawn into the protest by his older cousins and classmates. But he felt it too. He'd heard the whispers, carried the torment, and endured the taunts lobbed at him by his White classmates and the underhanded comments slipped into conversations by teachers. And, like his fellow Black students, he'd had enough.

In those days, Black students were bused into Tantallon, Nova Scotia, every morning from the historic Black community of Upper Hammonds Plains. The junior high school in Tantallon had opened its doors to Black students in 1974. By the late 1980s, when Lennett was in grade eight, there may not have been *public* protest from the White community against the consolidation, but covert racism was rampant within the school walls, nonetheless. Lennett wondered where his classmates had learned to be so cruel with their words and actions. What sorts of conversations were happening behind the front doors of White suburban homes in Tantallon? What generational racism was trickling down into the junior high school through muttered comments and harmful stereotypes? He didn't have answers, but Lennett was certain of one thing: he and his fellow Black classmates were not welcome.

And so, they staged a boycott. They refused to attend class. The media was called. Parents swooped in. Countless conversations took place behind closed doors. And perhaps the atmosphere shifted for a while within the school. Perhaps some eyes were opened to the lived experiences of Black students. But, as we look back from our vantage point in 2025, it's clear that there was—and still is—so much more to be done.

It can be difficult to admit that stories like this happened in our recent history, not some bygone era of generations past. But there are glimmers of hope in places like EBC: The MEETing Place, where the now–Rev. Dr. Lennett Anderson has been lead pastor since 1999.

In 2004, many years after that day on the school lawn, Lennett looked over his congregation in Upper Hammonds Plains as he prepared to preach. Just weeks before, *MacLean's* magazine had published an article that named him "one of five Canadian pastors who are breathing new life into their communities."[1] In response, attendance at the modestly sized African Nova Scotian church had doubled in a week, with people driving up to an hour to attend services.

---

1. EBC: The MEETing Place, "Lennett J. Anderson," para. 1.

"We thought they would only be spectators," Lennett recalled in a later interview. "But they stayed."

As he looked out over his congregation that Sunday morning, he recognized the parents of the White classmates who had told him he wasn't welcome at school, and the White teacher who had mocked the way he spoke, worshipping alongside his Black brothers and sisters. It was as if worlds had collided—past and present, then and now. Lennett didn't know what to do as this former teacher approached him after the service. What do you say to someone whose actions had produced a core memory of shame in your childhood?

"Do I hang on to this hurt and bitterness?" he asked himself, "or do I say, 'God, you are doing a new thing'?"

To his shock, she embraced him. "I'm sorry," she whispered into his ear, pulling him tight. "I'm so sorry."

"Only God could do that," Lennett said of the moment, tears in his eyes. "Only God could orchestrate this mosaic of believers."

Of course, God *was* at the center of that moment, moving through the service and the church in the following days, softening hearts as only he can. And, through the stirring of the Spirit, EBC had been working to prepare space for the people God would bring through their doors. This was not accidental. This was an intentional shift.

How did they do it? What steps did they take to move from being a historically monocultural, Black Nova Scotian church to the thriving intercultural congregation they are today? And what role did hospitality play in creating an ecclesial home where people from forty-four different countries are not only welcomed but celebrated and embraced with open arms?

KEEPERS OF THE FLAME

To understand the significance of the shift from being an African Nova Scotian church to an intercultural congregation, it is vital for us to understand some of the history of the Black church in

Canada and the historical resilience of Black people—specifically Black Nova Scotians.

The Exodus story has frequently been cited as an analogy for the migration of Black people to Canada. Propelled by the events of the American Revolution, Black Loyalists poured into Nova Scotia in the late 1700s, seeking to escape the proverbial Egypt and journey to a place where they were promised land and freedom. But long-established settlement patterns ensured that those promises would be broken. No land was given, or, if it was, it was very poor land "far enough out of [White] town[s] that they wouldn't disrupt the social life of the White people, but close enough so they could come in to work."[2] Separate Black and White communities weren't legislated—they didn't have to be. The colonial structures that guaranteed this separation were already in place.

While Black settlers were allowed to attend White churches, there were limits to how involved they could be. They were barely tolerated—pushed, over time, further into the margins of church life, relegated to specific pews and balconies, and eventually hidden behind curtains to satisfy the sensibilities of White congregants. Ultimately, this severe lack of hospitality, and even overt hostility, would lead to the establishment of monocultural Black churches.

Some ministers tried to bridge the racial divide. During his vibrant ministry, David George—a Black Loyalist in Nova Scotia— famously attracted people from both Black and White towns. But the hostility that ensued after he baptized a White woman was so great that George—and a third of the Black settler population in Nova Scotia and New Brunswick—left Canada for Sierra Leone.

"The [W]hite people of Nova Scotia were very unwilling that we should go," George wrote in his diary, "though they had been very cruel to us, and treated many of us as bad as though we had been slaves."[3]

Reflecting on George's ministry, Lennett sees George's life as a testament to the power of faith, perseverance, and inclusivity. "Despite the enormous challenges he faced, he remained committed to

2. Daniels, *Complex History*, 13:00.

3. George, "David George's Life," para. 18.

his mission of spreading the gospel and building communities not based on race but on faith," he says. "In the context of my leadership and ministry at EBC, George's legacy serves as an inspiring example of resilience, faith, and the importance of community-building through hospitality and service."

It was out of this resilience that the Black church was established in Nova Scotia and the surrounding Atlantic provinces. The Black church became a refuge when other spaces were hostile.[4] Congregations became family, extending hospitality to one another in ways they didn't experience anywhere else.

"The church gave us dignity," says Canadian poet and "Africadian" George Elliott Clarke. "It was the first institution that was able to do that. No matter how much humiliation people faced in their daily lives in the outer community in the larger world, they would come back [to the church] and feel dignified."[5]

Lennett describes the Black church as "the womb for Black literacy, entrepreneurship, and hospitality," a place where the community could let down their guard. Each person was celebrated, not simply tolerated.

It makes sense, then, that Black people put great value on leadership from within their communities. Former director of the North American Black Historical Museum Elise Harding-Davis puts it this way:

> We were the leaders, we were the conductors of the services, we were the ones who made the decision on what the congregation would study and how we would present ourselves to the world. Those of us who knew how to read and write took teaching positions in the church. We were educators. Church suppers were a way of learning etiquette. Everything we did had a learning component attached to it within the church.[6]

EBC: The MEETing Place is firmly rooted in this history of establishing sustainable, self-sufficient Black communities. The proudly

4. Johnson, "Heritage Story."
5. Daniels, *Complex History*, 3:31.
6. Daniels, *Complex History*, 28:15.

African Nova Scotian church has a rich heritage as a place of refuge, caring for the oppressed and forgotten, and standing united in the gospel.[7] Hospitality is at its core.

"Hospitality is a rich and multifaceted concept, deeply intertwined with cultural identity, historical context, and community values," Lennett says. "It is the beat of our drum! The African Nova Scotian community has shown remarkable resilience over the years, and hospitality here often reflects an adaptive spirit, welcoming others and extending support despite challenges and hardships."

The African Nova Scotian church was (and is) more than just a Sunday meeting space. It's a family center, a place of belonging, and a place where each person is treated with dignity. This is important because the generational trauma caused by racism is still intimately entwined in the lives of the African Nova Scotians who call EBC home today.

Indeed, racial tension continues to shape the social landscape of Upper Hammonds Plains in significant ways. In September 2024, the Canadian RCMP apologized to the African Nova Scotian community for the "historic use of street checks and other harmful interactions."[8] And even more recently, the citizens of Upper Hammonds Plains learned that fire hydrants in the community are unusable due to undersized water mains installed in the late 1990s[9]—a problem that would likely not go unaddressed in the historically White surrounding communities. "We are advocating for sufficient water infrastructure that guarantees community safety and has the capacity to meet current demands while supporting the growth and future vision of our historic community," Lennett says. As of March 2025, this is an ongoing and unresolved issue.

It is amid this messiness, this injustice, that the congregation of EBC extended—and continues to extend—hospitality to the wider world—indeed, to people who have not shared this

---

7. See https://ebcmeet.com/about.

8. Tremblay, "Nova Scotia RCMP Apologizes," para. 1.

9. Arif, "We Were Speechless."

experience of marginalization. We cannot overestimate the significance of this decision.

EBC, under Lennett's leadership, is picking up David George's mantle, intent on finishing what he started all those years ago in bridging racial and denominational divides. In this vein, Lennett encourages his congregation to be "keepers of the flame"—to walk through the doors their ancestors opened for them and to *keep them open* for others.

FROM BELONGING TO INCLUSION

Hospitality has been Lennett's guiding principle as he has led EBC towards becoming an intentionally intercultural community. But this has required sensitivity—a willingness to navigate understandable suspicions and concerns that others may take over or change the fundamental ethos of the African Nova Scotian church.

At the time of its founding, Emmanuel Baptist Church was a *community* church in the truest sense—most congregants lived within walking distance, and the vast majority were African Nova Scotians. However, when Lennett stepped into leadership in 1999, that dynamic began to change. Adaptations needed to be made.

One of the first adaptations was the church's embrace of commuting culture. People were now driving from various places around the province—within the Halifax Regional Municipality and as far as Lunenburg, Riverport, and Truro—to attend services. These newcomers were willing to make that commute once a week for Sunday services but not several times a week for traditional Bible studies and prayer nights.

Lennett had to ask, "How do we show up with a ministry of hospitality?" His answer? "We open our doors—whatever that looks like. We can't be guilty of what we accuse others of doing," he says. "We have to move beyond belonging to inclusion."

So, what did "open doors" look like for EBC? Somewhat radically for the early 2000s, the church shifted from on-site Bible studies to satellite small groups for midweek connection.

"I was a heretic in the eyes of some congregants," Lennett says. "Closing the physical doors of the church to midweek Bible study! It was unheard of." But he asked, "You may see the church doors closing, but do you see how many doors are opening?"

The church saw an explosion in midweek participation, with the "faithful fifteen" who had been showing up at the church building each week expanding to include over 90 percent of the congregation, now connected in small groups.

This sparked a bigger conversation about EBC's core values, which were ultimately defined as worship, excellence, service, unity, relationship, fellowship, and heritage—principles that continue to guide the congregation today. Establishing these values allowed the church to move forward in unity; metaphorical doors were flung wide to welcome the mosaic of believers from around the province whom God was leading to EBC. So deep was their commitment to hospitality that they decided to change the name of the church from Emmanuel Baptist Church to EBC: The MEETing Place—a safe community for *all* who seek to experience a true relationship with God.

Even after these successes—the commuter growth, the articulation of core values, and the embrace of a new name—there were still bumps along the way, mostly related to expectations. With so many people from different cultural backgrounds, what should the dress code look like? Which worship styles should prevail? Would traditional Black spirituals and gospel songs be swept away by the tide of contemporary worship music? Would the "talk-back" culture during sermons disappear?

Lennett modelled grace through these very real concerns, pointing people back to the mission: "to create places to meet," a mantra with hospitality at its core.

"I don't care what you wear!" he says. "I'd rather you be here than not."

Over time, new worship songs have been introduced, not to replace spirituals but to enhance them. Lennett has been pleasantly surprised by the depth these new songs have added to the worship experience, and he was moved by the willingness of others to learn spirituals and gospel songs as a staple of EBC's worship culture and heritage.

Initially, some new church members were put off by the "talk-back" culture of individuals affirming the preacher verbally during sermons, interpreting it as rude or disrespectful. But as grace was extended, and time was taken to explain the significance of this (very African) way of engaging with preaching, many embraced it—and now rival the volume and energy of the Black folks in the congregation!

What Lennett would describe as a defining moment for EBC, however, was when it came time to address leadership structure: "How are we saying we're a multiethnic church where anyone can belong, but everyone on staff still looked like me?" he asked. "Every deacon was Black and male. Not on my watch! I refuse to be hypocritical."

Over time, the church made intentional changes to better reflect those who are "in our house," as Lennett says. Now, when you look at the pastoral team, deacons, and ministers, you'll see people from different cultures, backgrounds, and experiences, all with a seat and a say at the table where decisions are made.

EBC's ministry has been shaped by an inclusion that embraces and celebrates diversity. "We want people to maintain their uniqueness in this context," Lennett says. "We want to be culture honoring and culture celebrating." Practically, this has meant empowering people to participate by praying or singing in their native language, embracing different styles of worship, and participating in cultural celebrations that resonate with the broader community.

"It means being attuned to both the challenges and joys of community members and responding with compassion," he goes on. "We're modelling a beloved community where we're different yet the same. We come together because we believe in equal opportunity, love for one another, and justice."

WOVEN TOGETHER

Lennett's approach to hospitality and interculturalism has been shaped in part by his heritage as an eighth-generation African Nova Scotian, but also by his deep understanding of Scripture, developed over many years serving in ministry.

"It is important to remember that individuals and groups discussed in the Bible came from diverse ethnic backgrounds," he says, referencing Acts 2:9–11 as one of many examples. "Even though the Bible does not talk about race in the same way we commonly use it today, it still has plenty to say about how people should relate to one another across cultural and ethnic differences. Throughout the Hebrew Scriptures, God's plan for salvation is built on the presumption of human equality and dignity and always assumes a multiethnic character. Scripture often speaks to *all nations*."

As we relate to one another across these differences, we are charged with extending hospitality, as Paul says when he describes the characteristics of a true Christian: "Contribute to the needs of the saints; pursue hospitality to strangers" (Rom 12:13 NRSVue).

As the stranger is invited in, as the doors are flung wide open in welcome, as all are included at the table and celebrated for what they bring, perhaps the church will inch closer to reflecting the "now" of the kingdom of heaven.

"God's fingerprints rest on everyone without restriction," Lennett says, "and all the people of God must be embraced."

If you were to walk into EBC: The MEETing Place today, you would find a table covered with a Kente cloth in the foyer, upon which sits an African Nova Scotian woven basket filled with a variety of fruit. These elements beautifully summarize Lennett's approach to hospitality and illustrate how EBC has embraced the changing face of its congregation. A sign on the table reads:

> This display reflects and celebrates the unique historical, cultural, and present-day realities of EBC: The MEETing Place. The colourful Kente cloth symbolizes the rich African heritage of the Black refugees of the [W]ar of 1812 who first settled in Hammonds Plains. In this new African Nova Scotian community, these pioneers, under the

direction of Rev. Richard Preston, established Emmanuel Baptist Church. The basket—an African Nova Scotian craft—represents the distinct worship style of the African Nova Scotian founders and their descendants who served this church for over 150 years. Today out of this African Nova Scotian context has emerged much fruit representing our multi-cultural, multi-racial, and multi-denominational membership and adherents. To God be the glory for this great thing he has done.

Heritage and history are neither lost nor forgotten amid change if that change is navigated with intention. The story that shaped the cultural identity of EBC: The MEETing Place is the basket cradling the future fruit of its ministry—a future of inclusion and hospitality extended to all of God's people. Let EBC and Lennett's visionary leadership, under the guidance of the Holy Spirit, be a powerful example of extending hospitality to create space for all who seek to experience a true relationship with God.

SUGGESTIONS FOR FURTHER READING

Daniels, Philip, dir. *The Complex History of the Black Church in Canada—Seeking Salvation—Religion Documentary*. YouTube, May 13, 2021. https://www.youtube.com/watch?v=81OFeofdksw.

Johnson, Allister. "Heritage Story: The African United Baptist Association." Acadia Divinity College, Feb. 15, 2022. https://acadiadiv.ca/heritage-story-auba/.

Sutherland, Arthur. *I Was a Stranger: A Christian Theology of Hospitality.* Nashville: Abingdon, 2006.

BIBLIOGRAPHY

Arif, Hafsa. "'We Were Speechless': Halifax Community Learns Fire Hydrants Non-Functional." CTV News, Aug. 20, 2024. https://www.ctvnews.ca/atlantic/article/we-were-speechless-halifax-community-learns-fire-hydrants-non-functional/.

Daniels, Philip, dir. *The Complex History of the Black Church in Canada—Seeking Salvation—Religion Documentary*. YouTube, May 13, 2021. https://www.youtube.com/watch?v=81OFeofdksw.

EBC: The MEETing Place. "Rev. Dr. Lennett J. Anderson, CD: Senior Pastor."
EBC: The MEETing Place, 2025. https://ebcmeet.com/users/rev-dr-lennett-j-anderson-cd.

George, David. "David George's Life." *Black Loyalists: Our History, Our People.* Black Loyalists, n.d. https://blackloyalist.com/cdc/documents/diaries/george_a_life.htm.

Johnson, Allister. "Heritage Story: The African United Baptist Association." Acadia Divinity College, Feb. 15, 2022. https://acadiadiv.ca/heritage-story-auba/.

Sutherland, Arthur. *I Was a Stranger: A Christian Theology of Hospitality.* Nashville: Abingdon, 2006.

Tremblay, Guillaume. "Nova Scotia RCMP Apologizes for Historical Use of Street Checks." Royal Canadian Mounted Police, Sept. 7, 2024. https://www.rcmp-grc.gc.ca/en/news/2024/nova-scotia-rcmp-apologizes-historical-use-street-checks.

DISCUSSION QUESTIONS

1. In what areas does your faith community need to demonstrate greater intentional hospitality? Are there opportunities for your congregation to creatively extend hospitality?

2. It's rare to see churches that openly acknowledge the difficult aspects of their past. What would it look like for your church to own its history, allowing it to shape current ministry efforts?

3. Are there subtle ways in which your faith community creates distance between your church and the surrounding community? What dynamics contribute to this, and how might you start to bridge that gap?

4. Take an inventory of ministries within your church that focus on justice. Is justice framed as a collective responsibility, or is it relegated to specific outreach activities?

9

Embracing New People and New Cultures in Traditional Congregations

STEVE MCMULLIN

To an extent that few congregations or church leaders anticipated, globalization and immigration have suddenly affected Atlantic Canada, as a disproportionate number of international immigrants choose to move to these four eastern provinces and as a surprising number of immigrants from larger Canadian centers choose to relocate to Atlantic Canada to take advantage of lower housing costs, shorter commutes to work, and the eastern Canadian lifestyle.

Socially, the sudden population increase in Atlantic Canada contributes to economic growth and helps with shortages in workplaces, most notably in the health care sector. At the same time, the population increase has led to a shortage of housing and a rapid increase in housing prices. For Atlantic Canadian congregations, the remarkable influx of immigrants raises important questions about how to welcome people whose culture and experience of the Christian church may be very unlike traditional Atlantic Canadian church life. According to Statistics Canada

(2021 census), the largest group of immigrants to Canada identifies as Christian,[1] and data from the Angus Reid Institute (2022) shows that immigrants tend to be more devout than Canadian-born Christians in practices like worship attendance, Scripture reading, and prayer.[2] The unexpected result is that some historic Atlantic Canadian congregations aging and dying five years ago suddenly find themselves with growing numbers of younger worshippers as they welcome devout Christian families from Africa, Asia, and South America. In some congregations, recent immigrants now comprise a large percentage of Sunday worshippers, and their children comprise the majority of those attending the church's youth groups and children's ministries.

The arrival of many immigrants and international students to Atlantic Canada in recent years requires congregations and their leaders to consider several important issues to ensure we truly welcome new people whose cultural backgrounds do not align closely with traditional Canadian church culture. That relates to immigrants with a strong Christian background in their country of origin and immigrants whose background is not Christian. How can Canadian congregations truly welcome and incorporate Christian immigrants? And how does a congregation graciously make disciples among immigrants who do not have a Christian background?

UNDERSTANDING KEY ISSUES
FOR CONGREGATIONS

The first obvious issue relates to church leadership. If a Canadian congregation is truly interested in incorporating immigrants into

1. Statistics Canada, "Religion by Immigrant Status and Period of Immigration: Canada, Provinces and Territories, Census Metropolitan Areas and Census Agglomerations with Parts," Statistics Canada, May 10, 2023, Table 98-10-0345-01, https://www150.statcan.gc.ca/t1/tbl1/en/tv.action?pid=9810034501.

2. Johanna Lewis, "Religion and Belief Among Immigrants to Canada," IQRA, July 12, 2023, https://www.iqra.ca/2023/religion-and-belief-among-immigrants-to-canada/.

church life, how soon does the congregation prioritize including people of different cultures in the leadership of the church? Does the congregation expect immigrants to "become like us" before they are included in the leadership structure? Is the congregation willing to listen when immigrants question or even challenge some traditional ways of doing church in Atlantic Canada?

A second obvious challenge relates to worship. How will we worship together as people from different cultures and church cultures? It is not just a question of how Canadians traditionally worship compared to how immigrants worship. Christian worship in India is not typically the same as in Nigeria, Brazil, or Korea. If an Atlantic Canadian congregation is multiethnic, will we encourage people to worship in accordance with their different backgrounds, or will we expect uniformity as the congregation worships?

Less obvious issues relate to being the church in a predominantly secular Canada. With Christians from a culture outside of Canada, there may need to be candid conversations about what it is like to live here in a predominantly secular society and about how it is difficult to reach secular Canadians with the gospel of Jesus Christ. That is especially important for recent immigrants who moved from a country with a more religious culture (whether predominantly Christian or another religion) and where spiritual dynamics are different.

When recent immigrants talk with me about their experiences of the Christian church in their home country, it sometimes brings to mind thoughts of what church life was like in Canada in the mid-twentieth century, when most Canadians attended church and many of the people who did not go to church thought they should. In the 1970s, I remember people passing out gospel tracts on the street corners of the town where I grew up, and I recall the evangelistic meetings each year in many local churches. Today, in a much more secular culture, such practices may be seen by Canadian society as cultlike, insulting, and perhaps coercive. However, recent immigrants may not understand these things, and they may think Canadian Christians have lost our evangelistic zeal. Of course, some Canadian Christians have lost their evangelistic zeal in this more secular time, but many Canadian Christians are seeking culturally appropriate and effective ways to reach their secular neighbours with the good news of Jesus Christ. At the same time, those evangelistic practices that now seem inappropriate to many Canadians may still be culturally appropriate ways to reach unbelieving immigrants because of their different cultural backgrounds. Those are examples of practices we need to discuss, because we can learn from each other. One of the things I have noticed at our church is a natural and genuine willingness among recent immigrants to invite unbelieving friends, fellow students, and coworkers to come to church with them. This can be very effective. These immigrants can teach Canadians some things about inviting others. Immigrants and lifelong Canadian church members and leaders can learn from one another as we discover our differences. It can be spiritually invigorating for everyone to see how culture affects how we follow Jesus and understand church.

A related issue is the potential loss of concern for outreach to secular Canadians. Some Atlantic Canadian churches are now growing, not because of disciple making or the effectiveness of the church's witness, but because of the influx of Christian immigrants. The church in Canada remains quite ineffective at reaching out to the growing number of secular Canadians, and it is noteworthy that according to the 2021 census, the second-largest group of recent immigrants also identify as secular.[3] If Christian immigrants enable local churches to maintain their size and financial health without focusing on reaching those who are lost, will congregations and leaders continue to neglect the Christian mission to make disciples among the increasing number of secular Canadians?

A final consideration for Atlantic Canadian church leaders relates to the cultural siloing of the Christian church that has already happened in larger Canadian centers. Congregations that are defined by the ethnicity of their members have become common in central and western Canada, and establishing ethnic congregations may seem much easier than including several

3. Statistics Canada, "Religion by Immigrant Status," https://www150.stat-can.gc.ca/t1/tbl1/en/tv.action?pid=9810034501.

ethnicities in a single congregation. Yet considerable sociological research indicates that such cultural siloing ultimately leads to losing most of the second generation from the church. Although immigrant parents may prefer to be part of a church that is culturally similar to their background, that may be a spiritual barrier for the next generation.

All of these issues require wisdom, change, and the development of new forms of hospitality. At Acadia Divinity College, I raised several of these issues in a sermon at a chapel service in February 2024. The remainder of this chapter features the text of that sermon.

"'CLONELINESS' IS NEXT TO GODLINESS, RIGHT?"

> Consequently, you are no longer foreigners and strangers, but fellow citizens with God's people and also members of his household, built on the foundation of the apostles and prophets, with Christ Jesus himself as the chief cornerstone. In him the whole building is joined together and rises to become a holy temple in the Lord. And in him you too are being built together to become a dwelling in which God lives by his Spirit. (Eph 2:19–22 NIV)

The sermon title is dating me, I am afraid. In the early days of contemporary Christian music, way back in the 1980s, just as I had begun serving as the pastor of two rural churches, Steve Taylor released a single entitled "I Want to Be a Clone." This song satirically extolled the virtues of *cloneliness* in church life, pointing out that once a person becomes a Christian, the church may pressure them to fit in—look, act, and think—like all the other churchgoers. What a crazy idea! Who would ever think that way? What followers of Jesus, having experienced the love and grace of God the Father, having been released from the bondage of sin by the resurrection power of Jesus Christ, and having been freed by the Spirit, would think that every Christian should be confined to being like everyone else in the church? Who would think that way?

Well, we can begin with Jesus' disciples in Mark 9:38: "'Teacher,' said John, 'we saw someone driving out demons in your name and we told him to stop, because he was not one of us'" (NIV). Jesus, you need to protect your franchise. You need to exercise some control—do you want to let just anyone drive out demons in your name?

Or we might think of the believers in Jerusalem when they heard that Peter had gone to the house of Cornelius and that the gentiles had received the word of God: "You went into the house of uncircumcised men and ate with them" (Acts 11:3 NIV). They are gentiles; they are not like us; they eat things we don't eat. What if more gentiles become Christians, and we become the minority? What if they start eating ham on Easter Sunday? No wonder they were concerned.

Or perhaps we remember Peter in Antioch, who freely associated with the gentile believers when he came to visit Paul until some folks from the church in Jerusalem arrived to check out what was going on (Gal 2:11–21). Peter suddenly stopped associating with the new Antioch believers with their sketchy backgrounds, to the extent that Paul had to rebuke him publicly for falling in line with what the old guard from Jerusalem expected instead of acting in line with the word of God. Even the apostle Peter ignored the word of God to fit in with what others expected of him.

The truth is that the temptation to be a clone is very enticing for Christians. When we are like everyone else in church and everyone else is like us—when we all worship the same way, act the same way, and have similar cultural backgrounds—we can avoid being challenged to think in new ways, and we can get by without extending grace when there are differences. We can avoid changing. But a major problem with that strategy is that, from my experience, my greatest times of spiritual growth have been when others have challenged me to think in new ways, when I have had to extend grace to people who are different than me, and when I have had to change my life in ways that I did not want to. Those have been the times when I have had to trust God most deeply and when I have had to follow the Scriptures instead of my own opinions. When I have seen God work in amazing ways through people who live out the Christian life differently than me, I have been reminded that Jesus Christ is Lord of his church.

When I look at the social changes in Atlantic Canada today, I am excited by the possibilities for the church of Jesus Christ. At the very time when spiritual vitality is at a low ebb in many Canadian churches, spiritually vibrant immigrants who are devout followers of Jesus are moving into our cities, small towns, and rural communities. At the very time when evangelism in Canada is stagnant, international students at our universities and colleges are showing a great openness to hearing and responding to the gospel. At the very time when not enough Atlantic Canadians are heeding God's call to pastoral ministry in local congregations, God is calling students from across the globe to study at Acadia Divinity College.

However, these new opportunities will be lost if we stubbornly determine that only clones have a place in our churches and that only those who fit our traditional Atlantic Canadian mold are welcome. The truth is, we need each other. New Canadians need to understand and appreciate the ways that God has worked and is working here in these Atlantic provinces. We have an amazing Christian heritage in this part of the world that can inspire us and encourage us all. But that doesn't mean that people of different cultural backgrounds have to fit into our church heritage and our ways of worshipping and living out our faith. Instead, they can share with us a vibrant Christian heritage of their own, demonstrate a dependence on prayer and faith in God that our churches need to regain, and challenge our often intellectualized, socially lifeless, and loveless ways of practicing the Christian faith.

These have been tough times for the church in Atlantic Canada. Too many congregations that were growing and thriving just a generation ago are withering and dying today, and one of the common responses of leaders in those declining congregations is a bunker mentality: "Let's freeze things as they are" or, even better, "Let's try to freeze things as they once were. Let's bring back the way things used to be, the way we want them to be. Let's strike the inactive members off the membership list instead of reaching out to them in love to see how the church has become irrelevant to them. Let's hunker down with the faithful remnant and keep things as they were." But there isn't much spiritual life in a church that is frozen in time. New Canadians can bring new spiritual life to these churches.

In our forty-three years of marriage, my wife Rosalie has gone to many baby showers. I hope I don't sound too uncharitable when I say I am "baby shower averse." Occasionally, an invitation would specify that a baby shower would be for both men and women, and I would make sure I had something else scheduled for that evening. But one Sunday at church, we were told that there would be a baby shower for a wonderful young couple who had moved from India a few years before. By then, the wife was serving on the deacons' board. We were told that they wanted us both to attend their baby shower, emphasizing the word "both." I politely declined as usual, but then I was told that they wanted me to lead in prayer at the shower. I thought someone else probably could have said grace before the lunch as well as I could, but I realized from their insistence that my attendance was mandatory. So Rosalie and I both went. I decided I could grin and bear it as long as I didn't have to play any of the baby shower games. We walked in to find quite a crowd—probably about fifty—mostly young men and women from our church. About half of those at the shower were fairly recent immigrants from various countries. There was more food than I would ever have anticipated; it was an amazing meal. After we ate, the emcee announced that it was time for prayer. She asked all those who had been asked to lead in prayer to make their way to the front, and about a dozen men and women from around the world, all in their twenties and thirties except for me, led everyone in a powerful time of prayer—at a baby shower! We prayed with our heads bowed for about thirty minutes—at a baby shower! The prayer time was the central event of the shower. This was not the usual Canadian baby shower. These were prayers characterized by faith, prayers of thankfulness, and prayers of love, sincere prayers from the heart. It was thirty minutes of wow, thirty minutes of being conscious that God was with us as we prayed. It was powerful, not only for the family that was the object of the prayers, but also for the many Canadian young adults who were witnessing prayer by their friends in a way they had never experienced in our Canadian *cloneliness* of praying. It was a powerful encouragement for me to see the sincere devotion of the international young adults who have become part of the fabric of our diverse congregation.

Young adults from Africa who are graduates of the MBA program at the University of New Brunswick, after they had been hired for their first professional job, asked me to come with them to the church parking lot after the worship service to pray a blessing on the car they just purchased. I had never prayed a blessing on a car before, and I have never had a young adult raised in Canada ask me to pray a blessing on their car, but I did so for MBA graduates from Africa. They explained that they wanted to thank God that they could afford a car in Canada, and they wanted me to pray that they would use the car for God's glory. Wow! In our Western materialism and consumerism, do we surrender our possessions to be used for God's glory? Is that part of our prayer life? Do we own our cars, or does God own our cars?

Those are just two examples of how my life and church have been enriched by people who do not follow Jesus exactly as I always have. I am not saying that Canadians need to start mimicking those Africans by having our cars blessed in the church parking lot, and I am not saying that every Canadian couple should have a thirty-minute prayer time at every baby shower, but I believe that we Canadians can learn much from the practices that people of other cultures bring to our congregations. At the same time, those people from Asia, Africa, and South America would be the first to talk about how their faith has grown in new ways as they have become part of the church here in Canada. We can help them understand how to follow Jesus amid a secular culture.

All of those thoughts bring me back to the Scripture that I read at the beginning of this sermon:

> Consequently, you are no longer foreigners and strangers, but fellow citizens with God's people and also members of his household, built on the foundation of

the apostles and prophets, with Christ Jesus himself as the chief cornerstone. In him the whole building is joined together and rises to become a holy temple in the Lord. And in him you too are being built together to become a dwelling in which God lives by his Spirit (Eph 2:19–22 NIV).

Paul was talking about a first-century church comprised of Jews and gentiles who, despite their significant cultural differences, were being built together as the church in which God powerfully dwells by his Spirit.

This time in Atlantic Canada presents a great opportunity for the church as we welcome immigrants from around the world in our midst and also as we seek to learn more about Indigenous peoples here in Canada. We have become increasingly aware of ways our Indigenous neighbours can teach us and help weaken the hold of individualistic, materialistic, power-focused Western culture on the church so that Jesus will be at the center—the chief cornerstone. We can welcome and incorporate people of other cultures fully into the life and the leadership of the church, not as foreigners and strangers, but as family—fellow members of God's household. May we, as the church of Jesus Christ in Atlantic Canada, open our hearts to the work of God's Spirit in this time and this place when he is bringing various cultures together in his church for his glory.

SUGGESTIONS FOR FURTHER READING

Lewis, Johanna. "Religion and Belief Among Immigrants to Canada." *IQRA*, July 12, 2023. https://www.iqra.ca/2023/religion-and-belief-among-immigrants-to-canada/.

Lingenfelter, Sherwood D., and Marvin Mayers. *Ministering Cross-Culturally: A Model for Interpersonal Relationships*. Grand Rapids: Baker Academic, 2016.

Livermore, David. *Leading with Cultural Intelligence*. New York: American Management Association, 2015.

Moreau, A. Scott, et al. *Effective Intercultural Communication: A Christian Perspective*. Grand Rapids: Baker Academic, 2014.

Statistics Canada. "Religion by Immigrant Status and Period of Immigration: Canada, Provinces and Territories, Census Metropolitan Areas and

Census Agglomerations with Parts." Statistics Canada, May 10, 2023. Table 98-10-0345-01. https://www150.statcan.gc.ca/t1/tbl1/en/tv.action? pid=9810034501.

DISCUSSION QUESTIONS

1. How can a Canadian congregation and its leaders encourage people from a variety of backgrounds to be authentic to their cultural identities instead of feeling they must change to fit into the Canadian church culture?

2. How can incorporating recent immigrants and international students contribute to the spiritual vitality of Atlantic Canadian congregations, and how can a congregation contribute to the spiritual vitality of people who are new to Canada?

3. Why do you think some immigrant groups form ethnic congregations in Canada instead of being incorporated into the life of existing churches? What are some concerns or limitations of having people worshipping only in culturally siloed communities?

10

On Hospitality as Public Witness

Resignation, Resistance, or Revival in Post-Christian Atlantic Canada?

D. STEVEN PORTER

AS GLOBAL FORCES TRANSFORM Atlantic Canada in the early twenty-first century, churches are noticeably absent from public conversations on the region's future. Given the ubiquitous presence of church steeples along the East Coast, the absence of a public religious voice is striking. Even if many of those steeples need a fresh coat of paint, they nevertheless recall a day not long past when churches routinely offered public leadership in local communities. From the 1780s forward, the lack of an official government designation did not prevent Protestants in the Maritimes, particularly Baptists, from functioning as the region's *de facto* religious establishment for nearly two centuries. Despite notable exceptions like the continuing prominence of clergy within the African Nova Scotian community or the call for assistance with refugee resettlement in 2015, civic officials now look to other sectors for leadership on local and provincial affairs.

The two most common Christian responses to this loss of cultural capital are resignation and resistance. Turning inward, some congregations lament the shift and resign themselves to operate more as chaplaincies serving their own members than mission outposts of the triune God. Others, turning outward, scramble to reassert the church's authority in the public square or, at least, to prove its continuing relevance to the political and cultural establishment. But this false binary does not exhaust the range of responses available to churches.

Instead of resignation or resistance, imagine what would happen if churches in Atlantic Canada embraced religious disestablishment as the best thing that could happen to their communities. That is, instead of mourning the loss of privilege or seeking its recovery, what if East Coast churches cast the remains of cultural establishment deep into the waters that surround them? Admittedly, for a people anxious about decline, this idea sounds counterintuitive, if not absurd. Some observers might even view it as an abdication of Christian witness. But unshackled from either the weight of responsibility for the culture's success or the burden of seeking its approval, churches in Atlantic Canada might discern in disestablishment a newfound freedom to follow Jesus beyond the main streets of their communities to the margins of society. And there, "outside the city gate," where Jesus dwells (Heb 13:12–13 NRSV), churches may discover new friends and focus.

This chapter argues that the rapidly changing profile of Atlantic Canada presents churches with an opportunity to revive their public witness through the practice of radical hospitality to strangers. To support this claim, the argument develops in three steps. First, we examine the changing context of public witness in Atlantic Canada. Next, we explore the practice of hospitality in the early church through the encounter of Cornelius and Peter. Finally, we consider how hospitality can revive the public witness of churches in Atlantic Canada.

THE CHANGING CONTEXT OF PUBLIC WITNESS IN ATLANTIC CANADA

Immigration

Many forces are transforming Atlantic Canada today, but the convergence of immigration, pluralism, and secularization holds special significance for the role of churches. First, whether people are moving to Atlantic Canada from other Canadian provinces or other countries, immigration is reshaping the population with immediate impacts on the employment, education, health, and housing sectors. Statistics Canada reports that all four Atlantic provinces posted significant growth in 2022–23.[1] New Brunswick, Nova Scotia, and Prince Edward Island all exceeded 3-percent growth, ranking them behind only Alberta for the largest gains in population nationally. Nova Scotia posted its fastest growth in over a century; in the past eight years the province has added more than a million people. With Atlantic Canada's largest population and its largest metropolitan area, Nova Scotia remains the region's bellwether. However, Charlottetown, Prince Edward Island, and Moncton, New Brunswick, have also appeared recently on lists of the fastest-growing cities in Canada alongside Halifax. But despite such growth, church attendance in the region continues to decline.

While population growth helps stabilize the economy, immigration also creates difficult challenges. Consider immigration's impact on housing and health care. Over the past decade, average home prices in Halifax have doubled. Depending on your situation, that increase may have improved your finances dramatically or placed home ownership permanently out of your reach. In 2022, Nova Scotia conducted a provincial housing needs assessment, which reported that 46 percent of renters and 36 percent of prospective home buyers were unable to find housing options within their price range.[2] By 2027, the report anticipates a shortfall

---

1. Statistical data is taken from Statistics Canada, the government of Canada's national statistical office: https://www.statcan.gc.ca/en/start.

2. Turner Drake & Partners et al., *Provincial Housing Needs Assessment*, 5.

of 41,200 housing units. Beyond affecting personal wealth, a lack of affordable housing also makes it difficult for universities and businesses to recruit students and workers. Shifting from housing to health care, it is no surprise that rapid population growth has also strained the health care system past capacity. In 2019, Statistics Canada confirmed nearly a third of adults in the region lacked a primary care physician, and its walk-in clinics recorded the longest wait times in the country. Beyond infrastructure challenges, immigration also impacts culture.

Pluralism

A corollary of the recent wave of immigration is the unprecedented growth of racial, ethnic, and religious diversity. In a region long characterized by limited immigration and cultural diversity compared to the rest of Canada, a rise in visible minorities—people who look different than the dominant race or ethnicity—provides a constant reminder of the cultural transformation of the East Coast. According to 2021 census data, 9.8 percent of Nova Scotia's population identify as visible minorities. Even though this figure marks a steep 6-percent increase since 2001, numbers alone do not convey the impact of the change as well as an illustration might. Imagine an art gallery hosting an exhibition of photography from fall festivals in Nova Scotia spanning the past two decades. In the pictures, you would see the increase in the number of visible minorities more vividly than any statistic. Of course, long-time residents sometimes welcome these developments, such as the growth of new businesses or an eclectic dining scene. But, other times, perceived differences stoke division within communities. When beloved traditions are changed, or the political and social status quo are disrupted, newcomers may face a backlash from long-time members of the community.

For example, church members already concerned with the waning public influence of Christianity on Atlantic Canadian culture may be wary of the religious diversity accompanying immigration from Asia and Africa. Such resistance, however, fails to acknowledge that churches were struggling in Atlantic Canada long before the government aggressively recruited immigrants. It also fails to acknowledge the deep Christian commitments many newcomers bring to Canada from the Global South, where Christianity is surging. To its credit, the leadership of the Canadian Baptists of Atlantic Canada highlighted the potential of immigration to revitalize local congregations at its annual convention in 2024. But it remains unclear whether local congregations will embrace that denominational vision. Likewise, in recent years, Acadia Divinity College has experienced a surge in enrollment of international students. Will East Coast congregations hire these students when they graduate? Notably, many of these students also arrive on campus with a passion for evangelism increasingly absent in traditional Canadian churches. This absence points toward the last factor transforming Atlantic Canada.

Secularization

Classic secularization theory held that the educational, scientific, and economic advances resulting from the European Enlightenment would lead to the decline and eventual disappearance of religious belief and practice in the modern world. It is difficult to dispute that Canada is experiencing a sharp demographic decline in Christian identification and institutions. Add public revelations of church-state complicity in residential schools, the clash between some churches and sexual and gender minorities, partisan activities of Evangelicals in the United States, and the rapid advances of science and technology, and religious faith looks increasingly out of step with the progressive sensibilities of a culturally diverse society. These factors have taken a toll on the reputation of institutional Christianity in Canada. But celebrations of religion's decline are premature.

Other evidence complicates the story of secularization's inevitable triumph over religion. For starters, while Christianity is declining in the West, it and other religious traditions are growing rapidly in other parts of the world. And even in the West, immigration continues to fuel religious growth in immigrant communities. Next, sometimes religions grow in public influence despite numerical declines. Consider the case of evangelical Christians in the United States. Historian Steven P. Miller describes a three-decade period starting in the early 1970s as "America's born-again years."[3] These decades witnessed the heyday of Jerry Falwell's Moral Majority; the elections of Jimmy Carter, Ronald Reagan, and George W. Bush, who in various ways represented Evangelicals from the White House; the Southern Baptist Convention's peak membership; and the rise of the megachurch as a cultural phenomenon. By the late 2000s, however, the number of Evangelicals in America and membership in evangelical denominations began to decline. Yet after a decade of losses, the election of Donald J. Trump in 2016 secured Evangelicals their greatest influence on the formal structures of American society through political and judicial appointments. Third, secularization theory also assumed that the only form of advanced society was one that looked like Western Europe. While that pattern may characterize Canada's development to this point, emerging advanced economies and education systems in the Middle East and Asia under religious and authoritarian regimes defy Western assumptions about what counts as "modern." The impact of immigration from those regions on Canada's religious future remains to be seen.

In sum, the forces of immigration, pluralism, and secularization reshaping Atlantic Canada present churches with an opportunity to revive their public witness in a post-Christian society. But this missionary situation requires more than a retooling of recent programming; it requires a fresh, Spirit-filled imagination, which leads us next to the book of Acts.

3. Miller, *Age of Evangelicalism*, 14.

HOSPITALITY AS PUBLIC WITNESS
IN THE EARLY CHURCH

The Acts of the Apostles recounts the development of the early church in the power of the Holy Spirit. Central to this story are questions of ethnic, religious, and political identity. Peter, a Jewish fisherman by trade, emerges as an early Christian leader following the death, resurrection, and ascension of Jesus. He advocates maintaining the distinctively Jewish character of the early Christian movement. Contemporaries like Paul want to push the boundaries of inclusion to admit gentiles into the church, but Peter opposes this move.

On its surface, the story of Cornelius and Peter in Acts 10 may not register as a story of hospitality. More often, readers associate the passage with cross-cultural evangelism, debates over gentile inclusion, and the role of the Holy Spirit in the early church. But hospitality emerges as a prominent theme across Luke-Acts and in this story. In *Saved by Faith and Hospitality*, biblical scholar Joshua W. Jipp studies divine hospitality in Luke-Acts, John's Gospel, and the letters of Paul. Across those writings, Jipp discerns that hospitality is a key attribute of the God of Israel, who not only extends hospitality to others but expects God's people to emulate this practice. Jipp also notes hospitality's reciprocal character.[4] For example, biblical stories often reverse the roles of guest and host. In the case of Acts 10, the story begins with mutual visions, involves mutual hospitality, and ends in mutual conversions. You may wish to review the chapter in the biblical text before reviewing the four observations below. The observations not only address the role of hospitality in a new missionary situation in the early church, but also raise questions for churches facing a new missionary situation in Atlantic Canada.

---

4. Jipp, *Saved by Faith*.

Observation One: Mutual Conversion

Many describe Acts 10 as the conversion of Cornelius. While this is true, Peter's conversion may hold even greater significance for the church's witness. In Acts 2, Peter addresses the crowd at Pentecost: "You that are Israelites, listen to what I have to say" (v. 22 NRSV). The sermon displays Peter's commitment to share the story of Jesus and his passion for God's mission to save Israel. But as Luke's narrative unfolds, readers discover Peter's convictions were insufficient conditions for apprehending the fullness of God's mission to the whole world. Peter needs a broader imagination, and the triune God employs unexpected means to impart one. By the end of the story, readers learn more about Peter's conversion than we do about Cornelius, but the greater lesson is that they need each other. Acts 10 depicts a mutual conversion that involves a mutual exchange of spiritual gifts. While churches in the West may be more accustomed to giving gifts than receiving them, the narrative of Acts repeatedly reverses expectations and practices. Outsiders become insiders. Benefactors become beneficiaries. Strangers become friends. There is no home base, no clear center for mission. The Holy Spirit moves in ways the followers of Jesus neither control nor anticipate. What sort of conversion(s) would such reciprocity require of congregations in Atlantic Canada? What preparatory work might this require of us?

Observation Two: A Missionary God

Acts 10 instructs followers of Jesus that the triune God always precedes the church in the world. Consider Cornelius. Although he is a pagan soldier and religious outsider to Israel, the Spirit has been working in his life long before Peter arrives in Caesarea. Even more remarkable, Cornelius is more receptive initially to divine revelation than the apostle. When Cornelius receives a vision, he responds obediently. At the outset, he may not be a disciple of Jesus, but he nevertheless fears the God of Israel, leads others toward God, gives generously, and prays consistently. For these reasons, the angel assures him that God has received his offerings and enlists him in mission (vv. 4b–8). By contrast, God must reenact Peter's picnic vision three times. Even then, Peter remains "greatly puzzled about what to make of the vision that he had seen" (v. 17a NRSV) and is "still thinking about the vision" (v. 19a NRSV) when Cornelius's entourage arrives at his door. Likewise, Peter's companions from Joppa are equally slow to catch on to the work of God in their midst. Luke reports they "were astounded that the gift of the Holy Spirit had been poured out even on the Gentiles" (v. 45 NRSV). Why were they astounded? Perhaps the temptation to locate themselves and their preferred guests at the center of God's concern is an occupational hazard for religious insiders. If so, how can congregational leaders cultivate a broader understanding of the mission of God in the world that neither undercuts confidence in the gospel nor mistrusts the rest of God's good creation? How might pastors, local clergy groups, and denominations prepare congregations to bear witness to the gospel with genuine openness and confidence amid the newfound religious diversity of their neighbours?

Observation Three: Multiplying Hospitality

Hospitality lies at the heart of this story and of Christian public witness. First, God welcomes Cornelius and Peter into a deeper relationship through divine visions. Peter's vision explicitly involves an invitation to table fellowship, which in the ancient world connotes religious intimacy. Although Peter still does not comprehend God's wider mission among the gentiles or even partake in the divine meal, he nevertheless reciprocates that divine hospitality when he welcomes the strangers at his door (v. 23). This act requires him to break the same Jewish laws of association he will cite the next day in Caesarea (v. 28). But housing three adult male strangers without warning also entails inconvenience, cost, and risk. What will the guests eat? Where will they sleep? As members of the occupying military force, what threat do they pose? At the end of the story, when Peter finally understands the wider welcome of a gospel without partiality, he shares the message and offers baptism, the basic rite of Christian inclusion (vv. 47–48). However, before Peter can even finish his sermon, God again extends hospitality by pouring out the Spirit on the gentiles with the same signs that accompanied the outpouring of the Spirit on Jewish believers at Pentecost (Acts 2:1–42). In response, the Caesareans invite Peter to stay longer. Hospitality begets hospitality and creates the context for gospel witness in this story. As the growth of cultural, racial, and religious others reweaves the cultural fabric of Atlantic Canada, how can churches practice hospitality with strangers?

Observation Four: Outside-In Transformation

The encounter of Cornelius and Peter is the story of an outsider's role in the conversion of an insider. Beyond complicating the meanings of "insider" and "outsider," it transforms the trajectory of Christianity from a tribal story to a universal one. This outside-in movement runs counter to how readers of Luke's Gospel expect the story to unfold, but it remains consistent with the surprising activity of the Spirit depicted throughout Acts. The Spirit working through Cornelius turns Peter's religious world upside down, expanding the gospel mandate beyond the Jewish community. Like Peter and his companions from Joppa navigating a new missionary situation, Atlantic churches may need to learn something about following Jesus from the people whom God sends them to serve—be they Christian or not. Thus, the practice of hospitality may consist as much in receiving gifts as in sharing them. And the humble act of receiving may have larger public consequences than congregations anticipate, whether mobs in the street, false accusations, or worlds turned upside down. Are Atlantic churches willing to be transformed by the Spirit from the outside in? Are they willing to risk marginalization through fellowship with strangers? If so, what structures or practices must congregations create to receive the hospitality of strangers?

With these questions in mind, let us consider the public witness of congregations at the intersection of our reflections on Atlantic Canadian culture and Scripture.

HOSPITALITY AS PUBLIC WITNESS IN ATLANTIC CANADA

Acts 10 offers a compelling example of what theologian Darrell L. Guder calls "the continuing conversion of the church."[5] While neither God nor God's mission changes, Peter does. The apostle comes to a deeper understanding of the nature and scope of God's mission beyond the Christian community—and that continuing conversion transforms the church and, ultimately, the world. Since Christians claim the same Spirit that animated the encounter between Cornelius and Peter remains on mission in the world today, then churches in Atlantic Canada have more interesting options than resignation or retreat in response to cultural change. But if Charles Taylor is correct, the longer the church labours within the structures of establishment, the more domesticated its imagination becomes. Following Jesus out of privilege to the margins of society, whether in Joppa, Caesarea, or anywhere "outside the gate" in Atlantic Canada, will be difficult work. This concluding section will reflect briefly on the challenge of public witness before considering the faithful preparation and risk it requires of congregations.

Notwithstanding the significant opportunities and gifts the convergence of immigration, pluralism, and secularization offers Atlantic Canada, a common cultural frame is not among them. Instead, those forces strain the seams of the fabric of East Coast society, which includes contributions from the Indigenous Mi'kmaq and African Nova Scotian communities. There is a correlation between the powerful forces impacting Atlantic Canada and impediments to hospitality. The second half of Joshua Jipp's study of hospitality in the New Testament identifies three primary obstacles to hospitality: tribalism, xenophobia, and greed. Instead of embodying radical hospitality expressed through friendship, reciprocity, and generosity, churches navigating cultural upheaval often seek to protect their insider status, maintain boundaries, and conserve resources. Such reactions quench the Spirit and undercut Christian public witness. By contrast, in *The*

5. Guder, *Continuing Conversion of the Church*, 91.

Gospel in a Pluralist Society, Lesslie Newbigin envisions a different model of congregational response:

> If the gospel is to challenge the public life of our society, if Christians are to occupy the "high ground" which they vacated in the noontime of "modernity," it will not be by forming a Christian political party, or by aggressive propaganda campaigns. Once again it has to be said that there can be no going back to the "Constantinian" era. It will only be by movements that begin with the local congregation in which the reality of the new creation is present, known, and experienced, and from which men and women will go into every sector of public life to claim it for Christ. . . . But that will only happen as and when local congregations renounce an introverted concern for their own life and recognize that they exist for the sake of those who are not members, as sign, instrument, and foretaste of God's redeeming grace for the whole life of society.[6]

Newbigin recognizes that the public witness of the church depends on the willingness of local congregations to eschew establishment and introversion in pursuit of a better city (Heb 11:13b–16a). While churches do not build the kingdom of God, they can bear witness to it by sharing their lives hospitably with others for the sake of the world.

Following Newbigin, a robust public witness does not require adopting a political program or the latest church consulting solutions, but it requires faithful preparation within congregations. As the observations from Acts 10 raised, what structures and practices do churches need to create to welcome strangers well? This can be as mundane as clear signage on property, or outreach in different neighbourhoods, or as complicated as learning new languages, hosting multiple services in different languages, or developing different ministry programming to meet community needs. The latter might drive a church to rethink the use of its buildings or its staff. At their core, such preparations involve reimagining the basic activities churches offer for the sake of others: worship and

6. Newbigin, *Gospel in a Pluralist Society*, 232–33.

prayer, meals, Bible study, fellowship, and mutual assistance. How might churches open such activities to the wider community, especially those on the margins of society? This openness is not merely a matter of marketing preexisting services more broadly; instead, it involves an openness to receive the gifts of strangers in such a way that they can transform the community from the outside in. Without that openness, the church is just another service provider among the helping professions that transforms strangers into clients, rather than a community of radical hospitality that transforms strangers into friends. Friendship may signify the most important change because friendship moves beyond charity to reciprocity and offers the possibility of mutual conversion.

Likewise, the language of friendship moves preparations beyond material activities or structures to questions of relationship and culture. What habits of heart and mind must congregations cultivate to rid themselves of privilege and open themselves to the hospitality of strangers? What cultural or economic blinders must we remove to recognize the new missionaries God has sent to the East Coast? Do we possess the humility to receive their hospitality? Will we accommodate different ways of viewing life and practicing faith within our congregations? To welcome strangers well requires a willingness to create space within the community for difference—whether models of parenting or expressiveness in worship. In 1 Peter, the author admonishes readers to adopt certain attitudes to strengthen the Christian community in a period of strain in the early church:

> Above all, maintain constant love for one another, for love covers a multitude of sins. Be hospitable to one another without complaining. Like good stewards of the manifold grace of God, serve one another with whatever gift each of you has received. Whoever speaks must do so as one speaking the very words of God; whoever serves must do so with the strength that God supplies, so that God may be glorified in all things through Jesus Christ. (1 Pet 4:8–11c NRSV)

While the source of strain differs, the dispositions commended are consistent with the needs of churches practicing radical hospitality today. Like Peter, churches in Atlantic Canada may find themselves the recipients of pagan hospitality, the pupils of foreign teachers, and the beneficiaries of friendships and other gifts they do not deserve. And like Peter, churches should not be surprised to experience internal resistance to such developments. Peter refused to receive God's provision three times, but the triune God is a patient teacher who can revive the public witness of churches in Atlantic Canada through human migration and even secularization.

Transforming congregations into communities of radical hospitality requires preparation, and it also involves risk. Privileging the needs of others sometimes means subordinating one's own. Friendship risks betrayal. Generosity risks poverty. But in Luke-Acts, the use of possessions is a key indicator of discipleship. As Jesus instructs his disciples:

> If any wish to come after me, let them deny themselves and take up their cross daily and follow me. For those who want to save their life will lose it, and those who lose their life for my sake will save it. For what does it profit them if they gain the whole world but lose or forfeit themselves? (Luke 9:23–25 NRSV)

Radical hospitality risks marginalization to follow Jesus.

In summation, I have argued that churches should embrace religious disestablishment and changing demographics in Atlantic Canada as divine invitations to reinvigorate the church's public witness through radical hospitality. Atlantic Canada boasts some outstanding examples of churches who have opened themselves to the hospitality of strangers. Their journeys have been inconvenient and costly, but also life giving, because they have led to mutual transformation. While other churches wax nostalgic for the past or worry about the future, those congregations willing to embody God's hospitality for the world will find renewal through the power of the Holy Spirit. By reflecting on hospitality through the lenses of East Coast culture, Scripture, and church practice, we discover that churches still have public leadership to offer their communities. However, such leadership will originate not from the center of culture but from its margins, where Jesus dwells alongside other strangers.

SUGGESTIONS FOR FURTHER READING

Jipp, Joshua W. *Saved by Faith and Hospitality*. Grand Rapids: Eerdmans, 2017.
Newbigin, Lesslie. *The Gospel in a Pluralist Society*. Grand Rapids: Eerdmans, 1989.
Okesson, Gregg. *A Public Missiology: How Local Churches Witness to a Complex World*. Grand Rapids: Baker Academic, 2020.
Root, Andrew, and Blair D. Bertrand. *When Church Stops Working: A Future for Your Congregation Beyond More Money, Programs, and Innovation*. Grand Rapids: Brazos, 2023.

BIBLIOGRAPHY

Guder, Darrell L. *The Continuing Conversion of the Church*. Grand Rapids: Eerdmans, 2000.
Jipp, Joshua W. *Saved by Faith and Hospitality*. Grand Rapids: Eerdmans, 2017.
Miller, Steven P. *The Age of Evangelicalism: America's Born-Again Years*. Oxford: Oxford University Press, 2014.
Newbigin, Lesslie. *The Gospel in a Pluralist Society*. Grand Rapids: Eerdmans, 1989.
Turner Drake & Partners, et al. *Provincial Housing Needs Assessment Report: Key Findings*. Government of Nova Scotia, n.d. https://novascotia.ca/action-for-housing/docs/provincial-housing-needs-assessment-report-key-findings.pdf.

DISCUSSION QUESTIONS

1. Is the loss of cultural standing and power a curse or a blessing for churches in Canada?

2. Are there differences between the hospitality commended by Scripture and the hospitality common to East Coast culture(s)?

3. What qualities, commitments, and practices do you think characterize hospitable congregations?

4. What activities, attitudes, and structures would your congregation have to change, to give and receive hospitality to strangers?

11

Welcoming the Stranger

The Stories of Canadian Baptists
of Atlantic Canada

JODY LINKLETTER

THIS CHAPTER WILL EXPLORE the experiences of individuals af-
filiated with the Canadian Baptists of Atlantic Canada (CBAC)
who have been involved in refugee sponsorships through their
churches. According to the 2024 yearbook, the Canadian Baptists
of Atlantic Canada have 418 active churches throughout Atlantic Canada. Since 2015, CBAC churches have sponsored more
than 2,000 refugees representing diverse nationalities and faith
groups.[1] What have been the experiences and stories of those
from the CBAC who have been part of welcoming individuals
to Canada? This chapter will share the findings of thirteen interviews representing fifteen individuals involved in refugee sponsorships related to CBAC churches between 2014 and 2024. First,
though, it will briefly examine sponsorship.

---

1. MacVicar, *2024 Yearbook*, 66.

REFUGEE SPONSORSHIP

The two main types of refugee sponsorships among CBAC churches are full private sponsorships of refugees (PSR) and blended visa office-referred sponsorships (BVOR).[2]

In PSRs, the sponsor selects the refugee(s), fully funds them, and provides all of their settlement support. This is the case, for example, with most family reunifications.

In BVORs, sponsors choose from a prescreened list of refugees from Canadian government visa offices. These individuals have been identified as refugees by the United Nations High Commissioner for Refugees (UNHCR). In this scenario, although the sponsor provides all the settlement support, the funding is split between the sponsors and government.[3] For some churches, this provides an entry into sponsorship.

To assist in settling refugees, the government signs sponsorship agreements with organizations called sponsorship agreement holders (SAHs) that participate in this process.[4] As one of 141 SAHs, the Canadian Baptists of Atlantic Canada assist churches in sponsoring refugees.[5] In this capacity, the CBAC can assist with "training, information sessions, and selection of a family for sponsorship."[6]

As an SAH, the CBAC initiated conversations with churches interested in sponsorship, most notably ignited by the Canadian Syrian Refugee Resettlement Initiative in 2015.[7] Many partici-

2. In her thesis on community refugee sponsorship, Rachel McNally outlines these and two other different models of sponsorship in Canada ("Community Refugee Sponsorship").

3. McNally, "Community Refugee Sponsorship," 9.

4. https://www.canada.ca/en/immigration-refugees-citizenship/services/refugees/sponsor-refugee/private-sponsorship-program/agreement-holders.html.

5. This figure is accurate as of Dec. 2024. In 2018 McNally reported that there were 106 SAHs in Canada ("Community Refugee Sponsorship," 10).

6. https://atlanticbaptist.ca/departments/refugee-sponsorship/.

7. https://www.canada.ca/en/immigration-refugees-citizenship/services/refugees/about-refugee-system/welcome-syrian-refugees.html.

pants interviewed for this chapter referred to the media coverage at the start of the crisis, as well as information sessions hosted by the CBAC, as sparking an interest to "do something" or to "make a difference."[8] To indicate the interest in sponsorship, for example, McNally reports that the CBAC "typically sponsored one family each year prior to the Syrian initiative. In 2016, the organization applied to sponsor 303 people, primarily through the BVOR program."[9] The BVOR option allowed an accessible path for churches to become involved in sponsorship and address a tangible world need.

Now that I have provided a brief overview of sponsorship processes related to the CBAC, I will discuss how refugee sponsorship is an expression of hospitality in the Christian faith and examine the experiences of individuals involved in CBAC sponsorship.

CHRISTIAN HOSPITALITY

Hospitality is commonly discussed in Christian circles and elsewhere. Many Christians understand that hospitality relates to their faith as demonstrated in the Bible, but it is also valued in the other Abrahamic traditions. Although much has been written about this subject, a helpful resource is Beth Nolson's dissertation, which explores hospitality as it relates to households of Christian faith.[10]

Nolson states that hospitality is core to Christian growth and is "an ancient practice employed by the people of God which extends God's loving welcome to the stranger."[11] She argues that hospitality is not just extending a welcome, but that it also involves holistic care for the other.[12] Through an extensive litera-

8. Many individuals referenced the coverage of the drowning of three-year-old Syrian Alan Kurdi.

9. McNally, "Blended Visa," 136.

10. Nolson, "Strangers at the Door." Also helpful is Soltes and Stern, *Welcoming the Stranger*.

11. Nolson, "Strangers at the Door," iv.

12. Nolson, "Strangers at the Door," v.

ture review and research, Nolson settles on a definition that can be applied to this chapter:

> Christian hospitality is a boundary-breaking missional activity in which God's welcome is extended to the *stranger* with no *expectation of reciprocity*. Unique to Christian hospitality is the conviction that having received God's hospitality *we generously extend it to others*. Hospitality modeled after the way of Jesus is a core practice of Christian discipleship which shapes practitioners as they embody God's welcome through cruciform practices of *self-giving love* that address physical, social, emotional, and spiritual needs. In a world of alienation and disconnection, hospitality creates safe spaces for healing through proximity, connection, mutuality, and authentic relationships. In our post-Christian context where Christian faith is suspect, hospitality provides a means for *demonstrating the gospel and the kingdom, and for partnering with God in* God's work of restoration, reconciliation, and transformation for the flourishing of the world.[13]

Earlier in her thesis, Nolson includes in her definition, "While hospitality is bounded by human finitude and limited resources, Christian hospitality is not thwarted by limits, but audaciously *trusts in God's abundant provision*."[14]

I have italicized key ideas about hospitality in the definition above that are supported by the stories shared in my interviews, as the following sections demonstrate.

EXPLORING THE TERM "STRANGER"

First, we need to ask, "Who is the stranger?" As Nolson discusses, "stranger" can refer to a wide range of individuals, including refugees.[15] Soltes not only argues that Abraham can be viewed

---

13. Nolson, "Strangers at the Door," 99; emphasis added.

14. Nolson, "Strangers at the Door," 47; emphasis added.

15. Nolson references the work of Pohl, *Making Room*, 6.

as a refugee but—amid his analysis of Abraham welcoming three individuals in Gen 18—also states, "The stranger to whom one ought to extend hospitality should not be viewed as a stranger, but as a human being as you, the host, are."[16] The refugee should be viewed as a human being, one who should be welcomed. Similarly, Participant 6 stated that "sometimes it is easy to see people from a distance from a label of refugee," but through the sponsorship experience, the individual discovers "how much people are people . . . just the depth of their hopes and dreams and anxiety as everyday full human beings."

The theme of welcoming the stranger is prominent throughout Scripture, and often Jesus himself is referred to as a refugee, since his family escaped for Egypt at the time of Herod (Matt 2:13). Soltes argues that we are called to not just welcome but to *love* the stranger and that "in the biblical context any stranger is almost certain to be of a different ethnicity and spirituality."[17] My interviewees indicated that those they welcomed were often of different ethnicities and faith backgrounds. Many shared that they stayed connected with their sponsored families well beyond the completion of their official commitment. The interviewees recalled being present during milestones with the families, such as births, graduations, and Canadian citizenship celebrations. A few participants also used the term "intimate" or family terminology when describing the type of relationships that occurred through sponsorship. For example, Participant 13 shared how two or three sponsorship families "almost became adopted [as] Grandma [and] Grandpa, because elders are really important to many refugees." The use of familial language to describe such relationships is also supported by McNally's research on sponsorship in rural Nova Scotia.[18]

In his chapter in this volume on hospitality and health, Glen Berry notes that although it might be easier to extend support to those who feel the same as "us," it may hinder the task of welcoming the stranger or foreigner as instructed by Scripture. Perhaps

16. Soltes, "Welcoming the Stranger," 12.
17. Soltes, "Welcoming the Stranger," 21.
18. McNally, "Blended Visa," 139.

some barriers to sponsorship relate to this idea, since many sponsored individuals have different backgrounds than their sponsors. Maybe fear, misunderstanding, and media make it easier to help those who seem more like us. Although some participants spoke a bit about unease with sponsoring strangers, this topic was not present in every conversation. Refugee sponsorship may be one way that individuals and CBAC churches can move past helping only those who feel like them to those who are different. It provides an opportunity to not just express a welcome to the stranger but to *love* the stranger.

NO EXPECTATION OF RECIPROCITY

The second point to highlight from Nolson's extensive definition is that hospitality has no expectation of reciprocity. Welcoming and loving the stranger, therefore, should not come with strings attached. In his chapter, Berry even argues from a health perspective that the benefits of hospitality seem stronger when there are no expectations of reciprocity. Nolson states, "Loving hospitality welcomes freely without coercion whereas exploitation offers welcome in order to meet a hidden agenda."[19] Interviewees discussed the tension that sometimes occurred when individuals had expectations of those they were sponsoring. Participant 12 stated that rather than approaching a sponsorship with specific expectations, one needs to have "an attitude to serve."

Participant 10 reflected that in the biblical story of the good Samaritan (Luke 10:25–37),

> there is no transaction, no expectation of anything in return. After telling the story, Jesus turns to the lawyer and says go and do likewise—this means that there is no expectation of anything in return for time and money. It was just one human to another. The image of God comes in—others are made in the image of God, and God expects us to treat them as such. We can give a cup of cold water without expecting a thank you.

19. Nolson, "Strangers at the Door," 38.

This participant understands that welcoming a stranger is part of the Christian faith and that we should not assume we will receive anything in return. This participant continues to reflect that this act of hospitality should be done because the other person is made in the image of God, and it is what we are called to do.

This concept of expecting nothing in return also relates to evangelizing. Not expecting refugees to convert to our beliefs is especially important since sponsoring churches are in positions of power. Participant 10 stated, "I insisted against—they were not evangelism possibilities. If they wanted to ask questions, that was fine. We couldn't evangelize [because of the] position of power." Being in a position of power means that those involved in sponsorship must not attempt to sway others to make decisions to please them. Nolson cautions that "hospitality without love is a dangerous practice, as it can be used for personal gain, abused by the powerful, and may exploit the already vulnerable."[20] Expecting conversion would make sponsorship not a form of hospitality, but rather a means to an end.

Although extending Christian hospitality should not be equated with overt evangelism, individuals may come to faith in Christ as they experience his power through shared lives, love, and God's care through sponsors. Reflecting on individuals who converted to Christianity, Participant 9 states, "They came to Christ because of the love shown to them." This statement can be an example of individuals experiencing God's love through the hospitality shown to them.

EXTENDING GOD'S HOSPITALITY
AND SELF-GIVING LOVE

This second point is closely tied to the third one: as Christians, we extend God's hospitality to others. Nolson discusses how God's hospitality is "boundary breaking," demonstrated through Jesus'

---

20. Nolson, "Strangers at the Door," 84.

welcome of many of society's outcasts.[21] The idea of extending God's hospitality is one reason that participants referred to sponsorship as important. Participant 8 stated that "hospitality and welcoming the strangers [are] more central to the gospel than we might recognize. Sponsorship bring[s] it to bear in an intense and special way."

Moreover, in her definition, Nolson explains that God's hospitality is seen through Christian's "self-giving love," which is modelled on the life of Christ. Participant 8 communicated that sponsorship is "selfless, generous service . . . it required a lot of selflessness, time and energy." Sponsorship was a way for Participant 3 to be obedient to God's call for extending hospitality. This participant stated simply that it was "just obeying what God says about hospitality."

DEMONSTRATING THE GOSPEL
AND PARTNERING WITH GOD

Flowing from this is the idea that Christian hospitality, in Nolson's words, "is a means for demonstrating the gospel and the kingdom, and for partnering with God in God's work of restoration, reconciliation, and transformation for the flourishing of the world."[22] Participant 6 discussed how their church had been "praying to reach the community and serve. This is getting dropped into our laps. Maybe [this is] what God is calling us to do. . . . [It] feels like a God thing to give us these opportunities."

This concept was expressed by Participant 8 in these words:

> It was positive for the church to see evangelism is sometimes bearing witness to the life of Christ by being incarnational ourselves, showing up in the flesh, dealing with the everyday life. It was very incarnational life for us to reflect on that—what does it mean to be like Christ to others? Jesus was rejected; we might be; it can still be good; it can still bear witness to the good news.

21. Nolson, "Strangers at the Door," 164.
22. Nolson, "Strangers at the Door," 199.

Continuing, this individual said, "We can't imagine what God will do—or how the witness of the church will bear witness through ... generations. . . . [Sponsorship is an] invitation to us to experience God's work in us and in the lives of family members." In different ways, participants spoke about sponsorship as a means of living out their faith in obedience to God's word, but also a way to be the light of Christ, a living hope pointing to Christ, to those who may not otherwise experience his love.

TRUST IN GOD'S PROVISION

The fifth point to highlight from Nolson's definition is that although we may not know where the resources will come from, we trust in God's provision. This was a common theme in my interviews. In speaking about the impact of sponsorship on them personally, Participant 5 discussed that, spiritually, "it was important to take that step of faith to make this commitment. We have seen God provide. The money always has been on top of the mind, [but] it has never been an issue or problem." They related that by subsequent sponsorships, there was a belief that "none of the things will be an issue; it will fall into place." Participant 5 further stated that through the experience of sponsorship, there was a reliance on God, an "understanding that God is a provider." Several interviewees shared stories of how God came through with money, accommodations, and other needs for sponsoring families. Participant 7 recalled,

> I saw God's handiwork so many times through the process: providing the right people for the task; free space to store all the furniture and donations; providing translators in the right places [a doctor who spoke the language of the family]; a house in the center of the community.

There was a sense of reliance on God to meet the needs that were required, even in private sponsorships.

IMPACT OF SPONSORSHIP

In addition to the five themes above, the next section will explore the impact of sponsorship on the participants, their churches, and their communities.

Personally

One of the questions I asked participants was the impact of the sponsorship on their personal and spiritual growth, their church and its members, and its relationship with the community. On the personal and spiritual level, participants discussed expanding their view of cultures and the world (Participant 2, Participant 6), becoming more hospitable (Participant 2), gaining a deeper sense of empathy (Participant 9), becoming more grateful (Participant 2), and becoming more connected to the church and community (Participant 7). Participant 4 discussed how they "never thought of multiculturalism until the sponsorship and now [are] excited to find out about new people and cultures." This same participant is now teaching English in their community. Participant 5 discussed how the sponsorship made them move outside their comfort zone and that it was spiritually important for them to take the step of faith.

Participant 8 further explained the impact of sponsorship on the individual participants, stating that it

> forced me to deal with my own selfishness [and] caused me to see the gift of Christ, in him coming to be with us—to see that in a new way and to recognize how I can be that for someone else—to serve them, generously. . . . There were times of pain and frustration—but more than that it has been helpful to grow the character of Christ in me—to practice Jesus in everyday circumstances.

For Participant 10, the personal impact was stated this way: "[It] hit me at the compassion level. . . . Having the family here and having to navigate the difference between religious traditions and cultures helped me to develop a deeper sense of otherness." And

138

Participant 13 shared, "It has been a blessing; it broadens your whole understanding of what Jesus was saying. . . . For some reason God chose for them to be within my circle, and I've learned a lot from them." The personal and spiritual impact of participants' direct involvement in sponsorship was evident in the way they spoke about their experiences. God used these relationships to change, shape, and leave a lasting impact on those who participated.

Church

It is evident that refugee sponsorship was personally impactful on sponsors. However, interviewees gave a mixed response regarding the impact on their churches. Participant 1 stated that it "did not have an impact on everyone, but [only] those that were involved." Similarly, Participant 3 was not sure of the long-term impact of the sponsorship on their church.

However, refugee sponsorship impacted other congregations more broadly. Participant 5 indicated that "the experience of welcoming refugee families . . . reflects how we are able to welcome those other international families to the church." After sponsoring refugees, other churches were described as more compassionate (Participant 6), as beginning English classes for newcomers (Participant 7), and as being more aware of (and comfortable with) cultural differences in the congregation (Participant 10). Participant 8 described the impact on the church in terms of a covenant relationship: "It challenged people to consider a longer form commitment in relationship. It forces you to deal with things you might be uncomfortable with. We are in this whether we feel good about it or not, like a covenant relationship. It is dynamic. This was a way that the people in the church could experience this other than marriage." Participant 6 stated that sponsorship provides an opportunity to deal with issues the church would prefer to cover up—perhaps cultural and religious differences—and it also has "changed how we pray and who we pray for." At least two participants discussed how their congregations have used their facilities for helping newcomers because of their experience in sponsorship. For several—but not all—churches, sponsoring refugees had long-term impacts.

Community

Participants likewise discussed how refugee sponsorship impacted their church's relationship with their community. Multiple participants talked about broadening their connections with individuals and programs in their communities (Participant 9, Participant 5). Participant 6 phrased it as "not [being] siloed into working with just people you agree with; working alongside other groups that are not church people." Participant 1 felt that sponsorship provided an opportunity for the church to be a light in the community and to become more visible. For some, the church became a place that was known to be collaborative. Participant 7 stated that "the church has become a place that other organizations contact for volunteers," while Participant 13 reflects that community organizations have called the church to help in other circumstances. Participant 12's church developed better relationships with its community, while Participant 10's church grew in its own "understanding of the community." According to interviewees, sponsoring refugees positively impacted their churches' relationships with their communities.

OTHER FINDINGS ON HOSPITALITY

During my interviews, individuals often demonstrated the impact of sponsorship through their facial expressions and the deep reflections they shared. Some recounted sad stories and hard times, such as walking with families through illness and grief; others talked about mental health issues and trauma that surfaced. Although there were challenges in doing life in relationship with the families, there was also joy. When discussing what they would say to someone considering sponsorship, Participant 8 said that others should prepare to "b[e] changed" themselves. As their experience proved, extending the hand of hospitality can be life changing.

Although they did not expect it, some individuals commented that they were also blessed by receiving hospitality from those they sponsored. Participant 8 stated that

> the act of receiving hospitality is a gift [and] important for us in the participation of what God is doing. Jesus often went to other people's homes for food and meals. He shows up and receives hospitality; that is a gospel witness as well. We were hosting them and we were also being hosted and experiencing God's presence as well. . . . It was humbling to experience the level of hospitality shown to me. They went above and beyond to say thank you or to welcome me in their home. . . . It was a level of hospitality I had not experienced from Canadians. The love towards me—that causes me to think and reflect more deeply what we do as Christians.

Participant 11 stated it another way:

> Financial wealth does not equal hospitality . . . many of the refugees that we have connected with [are] . . . limited in their material wealth, but they continue to offer hospitality to everyone who enters their home. . . . In our North American culture, we really don't generally offer the same kind of hospitality as is generously offered in many cultures around the world.

These participants were moved by the abundant hospitality of those they sponsored and encouraged to be more hospitable themselves.

CONCLUSION

As one who was invited to hear the experiences of those who have been involved with refugee sponsorship within the CBAC, it was a privilege to encounter stories of faith, compassion, and passion for everyone made in the image of God. It is clear from my interviews that interviewees became sponsors out of a call they sensed from God, supported by Scripture, to tangibly show his love and care to the world around them. Their stories impacted not just the participants themselves, but also those who have been able to hear about their experiences—how God has been present and active through each of them.

Many participants were impacted by simply knowing that they had made a difference for not just one generation, but also for those to come. Others were touched by the generosity and hospitality shown to them by their sponsored families. Still other participants, but not all, recounted how sponsorship has made their church more open to those of different cultures and nationalities. When asked what they would say to others considering sponsorship, interviewees conveyed messages such as "Go for it!," "Do it," "It's rewarding," "You will not regret doing it," "It's hard work," along with other practical advice such as "counting the cost," "remember[ing] that refugees did not choose to leave their homes," and "doing their homework on differences [cultural, food, language]." Participant 8 summed up the experience of sponsorship in words with which other participants would likely agree: "A gift and a beautiful thing to be part of."

SUGGESTIONS FOR FURTHER READING

McNally, Rachel. "Community Refugee Sponsorship and Integration in Rural Nova Scotia." Undergraduate honors thesis, Acadia University, 2018.

Nolson, Beth. "Strangers at the Door: Extending God's Welcome Through Household Hospitality." Doctor of Practical Theology diss., McMaster Divinity College, 2023.

Soltes, Ori Z., and Rachel Stern, eds. Welcoming the Stranger: Abrahamic Hospitality and Its Contemporary Implications. New York: Fordham University Press, 2024.

BIBLIOGRAPHY

MacVicar, Renée, ed. 2024 Yearbook. Moncton, NB: Canadian Baptists of Atlantic Canada, 2024. https://baptist-atlantic.ca/news/cbac-news/2024-yearbook-available-for-download/.

McNally, Rachel. "The Blended Visa Office-Referred Program." In *Strangers to Neighbours: Refugee Sponsorship in Context*, edited by Shauna Labman and Geoffrey Cameron, 134–51. Refugee and Forced Migration Studies 3. Montreal: McGill-Queen's University Press, 2020.

———. "Community Refugee Sponsorship and Integration in Rural Nova Scotia." Undergraduate honors thesis, Acadia University, 2018.

Nolson, Beth. "Strangers at the Door: Extending God's Welcome Through Household Hospitality." Doctor of Practical Theology diss., McMaster Divinity College, 2023.

Pohl, Christine D. *Making Room: Recovering Hospitality as a Christian Tradition.* Grand Rapids: Eerdmans, 1999.

Soltes, Ori Z. "Welcoming the Stranger in the Jewish Tradition." In *Welcoming the Stranger: Abrahamic Hospitality and Its Contemporary Implications*, edited by Ori Z. Soltes and Rachel Stern, 11–25. New York: Fordham University Press, 2024.

DISCUSSION QUESTIONS

1. Before reading this chapter, had you considered sponsoring refugee families to be an expression of Christian hospitality? Why or why not?

2. When you think of hospitality in Scripture, which passages or stories come to mind? Discuss some of the implications of these passages. How might they connect to the themes of this chapter, as well as to your own life?

3. Revisit Nolson's definition of Christian hospitality presented at the beginning of the chapter. What aspects of her definition surprised or challenged you? Why? Do you agree that hospitality "is a core practice of Christian discipleship"? Why or why not?

4. What part of extending Christian hospitality to refugees do you think would be the most challenging for you personally? Reflect on why this might be difficult.

5. How have some of the stories in this chapter inspired you to extend hospitality to the stranger?

www.ingramcontent.com/pod-product-compliance
Lightning Source LLC
Chambersburg PA
CBHW070921270326
41927CB00011B/2676